WITHDRAWN

The War of Desire and Technology
at the Close of the Mechanical Age

The War of Desire and Technology
at the Close of the Mechanical Age

Allucquère Rosanne Stone

The MIT Press
Cambridge, Massachusetts
London, England

This book was set in Sabon by Achorn Graphic Services and was printed and bound in the United States of America.

Library of Congress Cataloging-in-Publication Data
Stone, Allucquère Rosanne.
   The war of desire and technology at the close of the mechanical age / Allucquère Rosanne Stone.
     p. cm.
   Includes bibliographical references.
   ISBN 0-262-19362-0
   1. Computers and civilization. 2. Virtual reality. 3. Information technology. I. Title.
QA76.9.C66S883 1995
303.48'34—dc20
                                      95–17286
                                          CIP

This book is dedicated to the memory of Nathaniel and Mathilde Fisher, Murry Glasser, and Robert Ensel, whose faith and support made it possible.

Contents

Acknowledgments

Over the relatively short time in which I've been pursuing this work I have met an astonishing number of fascinating and talented people, more than one of whom has affected my life in significant ways.

In The Beginning was Billie Harris, both executive and den mother par excellence, who cared enough to make my return to the academic world possible. Stephanie Valkyrie introduced me to my first phone sex experience, and sat patiently while I tried to figure it out. Bandit Gangwere gave me my first entry to an important community of engineers. Jon Singer, who knows everybody and cooks everything and of whom Vonda MacIntyre says, "Yes, folks, I know him too," introduced me to damn near everyone in the sidereal universe, as well as managing to put me in touch with St-John Perse, the wonderful quasiguy who sits patiently on my desk year after year and who is still among my closest friends.

Michael Benedikt invited me to the First Conference on Cyberspace and, besides having astonishing insights into the nature of virtuality, not only abetted my move to Austin but has put up with me ever since. Brenda Laurel, one of the most ripping sharp people who has ever crossed my path, has been a source of so many jolting insights that I can't begin to sort them out. Her love and friendship have been invaluable. Avital Ronell shared insights, walks on the beach, and important visions. Sherry Turkle, Thomas Kuhn, Clifford Geertz, Richard Rorty, and Charles Taylor were kind enough to extend an ear or a hand before anybody had ever heard of virtual systems.

Sanford Kwinter was unfailingly encouraging and farsighted. Anselm Strauss' kind humor has been immensely encouraging.

Mischa Adams, Chela Sandoval, John James, Scott Fisher, Pavel Curtis, Barbara Joans, Sharon Traweek, Gloria Anzaldúa, Adele Clarke, Alan Wexelblat, Roddey Reid, Seena Frost, Kristina Straub, Julia Epstein, Marilyn and Art Russell, and Myrtle Ensel have been of great help, and Thyrza Goodeve's insights about the interplay of body and memory have been invaluable. Kate Bornstein, playwright and performer, gave me renewed courage at a critical time. Susan Leigh Star was largely responsible for pointing me back toward the academic world when I had wandered happily but stupidly afield, and provided much material and inspiration for my three science fiction novels-in-progress.

My colleagues in the Department of Radio, TV and Film at the University of Texas at Austin, and in particular our Chair, John Downing, have been thoroughly and blessedly supportive during the latter stages. The students, faculty, and especially the enthusiastic cyberhackers who have rallied around the Advanced Communication Technologies Laboratory (ACTLab), including the designers and operators of the ACTLab's first experimental virtual social communities ACTMUD, MUMOO, and PointMOOt Texas, have recharged my batteries and turned my props. Wendy Brown provided unquestioning support and excellent advice for the Second International Conference on Cyberspace, which brought together for the first time many of the people whose work has been pivotal for my own. Sandra Dijkstra, literary agent without peer, is the real hand at the tiller. And Bob Prior at MIT Press has been a kind listener and gentle guide from the time when the text was in as virtual a form as a textual production is likely to get. Faith like that can move mountains, Hallelujah.

Finally, Donna Haraway. *Ave Mater Gloriosa*. And *Alana Ktahmet moy senyo nui hgytah,* for good measure.

Allucquère Rosanne Stone

Collective structures . . . reproduce themselves historically by risking themselves in novel conditions. Their wholeness is as much a matter of reinvention and encounter as it is of continuity and survival.

—James Clifford

A group constituted around a common symbolic structure is a "culture area" of its own, the limits of which are set neither by territory nor formal membership, but by the limits of effective communication.

—Anselm Strauss

The subjects are cyborg, nature is Coyote, and the geography is Elsewhere.

—Donna Haraway

Introduction: Sex, Death, and Machinery, or How I Fell in Love with My Prosthesis

It started this afternoon when I looked down at my boots. I was emerging from a stall in the women's room in my department. The university was closed for the holidays. The room was quite silent except for the distant rush of the air conditioning, imparting to the cramped institutional space the mechanical qualities of a submarine. I was idly adjusting my clothing, thinking of nothing in particular, when I happened to look down, and there they were: My boots. Two completely unremarkable boots. They were right where they belonged, on the ends of my legs. Presumably my feet were inside.

I felt a sudden thrill of terror.

Maybe, I suppose, the boots could have reminded me of some long-buried trauma, of the sort that Freudians believe leads to shoe fetishism. But my sudden fear was caused by something quite different. What was driving me was not the extraordinariness of the sight of my own boots, but the ordinariness of them. They were common as grass. In fact, I realized that I hadn't even thought about putting them on. They were *just there*. If you wanted to "get real ugly about it"— as they say in Austin—you might call it a moment of radical existential *Dasein*, in the same way you might say déjà vu again. I had become transparent to myself. Or rather, the *I* that I customarily express and that reflexively defines me through my chosen personal style had become part of the wallpaper.

This is hardly a serious problem for some. But I tend to see myself as an entity that has chosen to make its life career out of playing with identity. It sometimes seems as though everything in my past has been a kind of extended excuse for experiments with subject position and interaction. After all, what material is better to experiment with than one's self? Academically speaking, it's not exactly breaking new ground to say that any subject position is a mask. That's well and good, but still most people take some primary subject position for granted. When pressed, they may give lip service to the idea that perhaps even their current "root" persona is also a mask, but nobody really believes it. For all intents and purposes, your "root" persona is *you*. Take that one away, and there's nobody home.

Perhaps someone with training in drama already perceives this, but it was a revelation to me. In the social sciences, symbolic interactionists believe that the root persona is always a momentary expression of ongoing negotiations among a horde of subidentities, but this process is invisible both to the onlooker and to the persona within whom the negotiations are taking place. For me this has never been particularly true. My current *I* has been as palpably a mask to me as any of my other *I*'s have been. Perceiving that which is generally invisible as really a kind of capital has been more than a passing asset (as it were); it has been a continual education, a source of endless challenge, not to mention fear, and certainly not least, an ongoing celebration of the sacred nature of the universe of passing forms. It was for these reasons, then, that I found looking down rather complacently at my boots and not really seeing them to be so terrifying. Like an athlete who has begun to flub a long-polished series of moves, I began to wonder if I was losing my edge.

Going through life with this outlook has been a terrific asset in my chosen work, and the current rise in the number of people who engage in social interactions without ever meeting in the customary sense of the term—that is, engaging in social intercourse by means of communication technologies—has given me increasing opportunities to watch others try on their own alternative personae. And although most still see those personae as just that—alternatives to a customary "root" identity—there are some out at the margins who have always lived comfortably with the idea of floating identities, and inward from the margins there are a few who are beginning, just a bit, to question. What it is they are questioning is a good part of what this essay is about.

A bit of background may be appropriate here.

I have bad history: I am a person who fell in love with her own prostheses. Not once, but twice. Then I fell in love with somebody *else's* prosthesis.

The first time love struck was in 1950. I was hunkered down in the dark late at night, on my bed with the big iron bedstead on the second floor, listening absently to the crickets singing and helping a friend scratch around on the surface of a galena crystal that was part of a primitive radio. We were looking for one of the hot spots, places where the crystal had active sites that worked like diodes and could detect radio waves. There was nothing but silence for a long, long time, and then suddenly the earphones burst into life, and a whole new universe was raging in our heads—the ranting voice of Jean Shepherd, boiling into the atmosphere from the massive transmitter of WOR-AM, 50 kilowatts strong and only a few miles away. At that distance we could have heard the signal in our tooth fillings if we'd had any, but the transmitter might as well have been in Rangoon, for all the fragrant breath of exotic worlds it suggested. I was hooked. Hooked on technology. I could take a couple of coils of wire and a hunk of galena and send a whole part of myself out into the ether. An extension of my will, of my instrumentality . . . that's a prosthesis, all right.

The second time happened in 1955, while I was peering over the edge of a 24 24 recording console. As I stood on tiptoe, my nose just clearing the top of the console, from my age and vantage point the massive thing looked as wide as a football field. Knobs and switches from hell, all the way to the horizon . . . there was something about that vast forest of controls that suggested the same breath of exotic worlds that the simple coil of wire and the rickety crystal did.

I was hooked again. Hooked on even bigger technology, on another extension of my instrumentality. I could create whole oceans of sound, universes of sound, could at last begin on my life's path of learning how to make people laugh, cry, and throw up in dark rooms. And I hadn't even heard it turned *on*.[1]

But the third time . . .

The third time was when Hawking came to town.

Stephen Hawking, the world-famous physicist, was giving a lecture at UC Santa Cruz. The auditorium was jammed, and the overflow crowd was being accommodated outside on the lawn. The lawn looked like a medieval fair, with people sitting on blankets and towels, others standing or milling around, all ears cocked toward the loudspeakers that were broadcasting Hawking's address across the landscape.

If you haven't seen Stephen Hawking give a talk, let me give you a quick background. Hawking has amyotrophic lateral sclerosis, which makes it virtually impossible for him to move anything more than his fingers or to speak. A friendly computer engineer put together a nice little system for him, a program that displays a menu of words, a storage buffer, and a Votrax allophone generator—that is, an artificial speech device. He selects words and phrases, the word processor stores them until he forms a paragraph, and the Votrax says it. Or he calls up a prepared file, and the Votrax says that.

So I and a zillion other people are on the lawn, listening to Hawking's speech, when I get the idea that I don't want to be outside with the PA system—what I really want to do is sneak into the auditorium, so I can actually hear Hawking give the talk.

In practice this maneuver proves not too hard. The lecture is under way, security is light—after all, it's a *physicist,* dammit, not the UC Board of Regents, for which they would have had armed guards with two-way radios—so it doesn't take long for me to worm my way into the first row.

And there is Hawking. Sitting, as he always does, in his wheelchair, utterly motionless, except for his fingers on the joystick of the laptop;

and on the floor to one side of him is the PA system microphone, nuzzling into the Votrax's tiny loudspeaker.

And a thing happens in my head. Exactly where, I say to myself, *is* Hawking? Am I any closer to him now than I was outside? Who is it doing the talking up there on stage? In an important sense, Hawking doesn't stop being Hawking at the edge of his visible body. There is the obvious physical Hawking, vividly outlined by the way our social conditioning teaches us to see a person as a person. But a serious part of Hawking extends into the box in his lap. In mirror image, a serious part of that silicon and plastic assemblage in his lap extends into him as well . . . not to mention the invisible ways, displaced in time and space, in which discourses of medical technology and their physical accretions already permeate him and us. No box, no discourse; in the absence of the prosthetic, Hawking's intellect becomes a tree falling in the forest with nobody around to hear it. On the other hand, with the box his voice is auditory and simultaneously electric, in a radically different way from that of a person *speaking* into a microphone. Where *does* he stop? Where are his edges? The issues his person and his communication prostheses raise are boundary debates, borderland/*frontera* questions. Here at the close of the mechanical age, they are the things that occupy a lot of my attention.[2]

Flashback: I Was Idly Looking

I was idly looking out my window, taking a break from some nasty piece of academic writing, when up the dusty, rutted hill that constitutes my driveway and bastion against the world there abruptly rode, on a nasty little Suzuki Virago, a brusque, sharp-tongued person of questionable sexuality. Doffing her helmet, she revealed herself, both verbally and physically, as Valkyrie, a postoperative m/f transgender with dark hair and piercing black eyes who evinced a pronounced affinity for black leather. She announced that there were things we had to do and places we had to go, and before I could mutter "science fiction" we were off on her bike.[3]

Valkyrie proceeded to introduce me to a small community of women in the San Francisco Bay area. Women's collectives were not new to me; I had recently studied a group of women who ran a business, housed themselves under one roof, and lived their lives according to the principles of a canonically undefined but quite powerful idea known as lesbian separatism.[4] But the group to which my new friend now introduced me did not at all fit the model I had painstakingly learned to recognize. This collective ran a business, and the business was hetero phone sex . . . not something of which my other research community, immured in radical lesbian orthodoxy, would have approved.

I was instantly entranced, and also oddly repelled. After all, I had broken bread with one of the most episcopal of women's collectives for five years, and any deviation from group norms would have been punishable in fairly horrid ways. To imagine that hetero sex could be enjoyable, not to mention profitable, was playing into the hands of the gentiles, and even to spend time with a group that supported itself in such a manner (and even joked about it) could have had mortal consequences.

For reasons best described as kismet, the phone sex workers and I became good friends. We found each other endlessly fascinating. They were intrigued by my odd history and by what I'd managed to make out of it. In turn, I was intrigued by the way they negotiated the mine fields of ethics and personal integrity while maintaining a lifestyle that my other research community considered unthinkable.

After a while, we sorted out two main threads of our mutual attraction. From my point of view, the more I observed phone sex the more I realized I was observing very practical applications of data compression. Usually sex involves as many of the senses as possible. Taste, touch, smell, sight, hearing—and, for all I know, short-range psychic interactions—all work together to heighten the erotic sense. Consciously or unconsciously phone sex workers translate all the modalities of experience into audible form. In doing so they have reinvented the art of radio drama, complete down to its sound effects, including the fact that some sounds were best represented by *other* improbable sounds that they resembled only in certain iconic ways. On the radio, for example, the soundmen (they were always literally men) represented fire by crumpling cellophane, because to the audience it sounded *more like* fire than holding a microphone to a real fire did.

The sex workers did similar stuff. I made a little mental model out of this: The sex workers took an extremely complex, highly detailed set of behaviors, translated them into a single sense modality, then further boiled them down to a series of highly compressed tokens. They then squirted those tokens down a voice-grade phone line. At the other end of the line the recipient of all this effort added boiling water, so to speak, and reconstituted the tokens into a fully detailed set of images and interactions in multiple sensory modes.

Further, what was being sent back and forth over the wires wasn't just information, it was *bodies*. The majority of people assume that erotics implies bodies; a body is part of the idea of erotic interaction and its concomitants, and the erotic sensibilities are mobilized and organized around the idea of a physical body which is the seat of the whole thing. The sex workers' descriptions were invariably and quite directly about physical bodies and what they were doing or what was being done to them.

Later I came to be troubled by this focus on bodies because of its relation to a remark of Elaine Scarry's. In a discussion of human experience in her book *The Body in Pain*, she says,

Pain and imagining are the "framing events" within whose boundaries all other perceptual, somatic, and emotional events occur; thus, between the two extremes can be mapped the whole terrain of the human psyche (165).

By that time I had stopped thinking of the collective as a group of sex workers and had begun to think of them in rather traditional anthropological terms as *my* sex workers. I had also moved on to a more complex mode of fieldwork known as participant observation, and I was getting an education I hadn't expected. Their experience of the world, their ethical sense, the ways they interpreted concepts like work and play were becoming part of my own experience. I began to think about how I could describe them in ways that would make sense to a casual reader. As I did so, Scarry's remark returned to intrigue me because of its peculiar relationship to the social groups I was studying. It seemed to me that the sex workers' experiential world was organized in a way that was almost at right angles to Scarry's description of the continuum of pain and imagining. The world of the sex workers and their clients, I observed, was not organized along a continuum of pain and imagination but rather within an experiential field in which *pleasure* and imagination were the important attractors.

Patently it is not difficult in these times to show how phone sex interactions take place within a field of power by means of which desire comes to have a particular shape and character. In the early days of phone sex that view would have been irrefutable, but things are changing rather fast in the phone sex business; more traditional hetero and hetero-modeled interactions may still get their kick from very old patterns of asymmetrical power, but there seems little doubt that the newer forums for phone sex (as well as other forms of technologically mediated human interaction) have made asymmetrical power relationships part of a much larger and more diverse erotic and experiential tool kit.

This diversity has obvious and interesting implications for critical studies, but it does not in any way imply that a hypothetical "new erotics," if that's what I'm describing, has escaped from the bottomless gravity well of the same power structures within which we find ourselves fixed in position, regardless of what our favorite position is. It does seem to mean, though, that a good many of the people I observe are aware of the effects of those structures, even though as of this writing I see little effort to alter or transcend them. There does appear to be a central and critical reason for this lack of effort, particularly in regard to erotics, and that is that none of the people

I observe who *do* erotics—even those who play with different structures of power—have yet begun to speculate on how erotics really works.

There are other areas of inquiry which are organized around what might be called an epistemological Calvinism. A recent but fairly broad area of inquiry in the social sciences into the nature and character of human-computer interaction is known as the study of computer-supported cooperative work (CSCW). Part of the informing philosophy of this discipline is the idea that all human activity can be usefully interpreted as a kind of work, and that work is the quintessential defining human capacity. This, too, I think, misses some of the most important qualities of human-computer interaction just as it does when applied to broader elements of human experience. By this I mean that a significant part of the time that humans spend in developing interactional skills is devoted not to work but to what by common understanding would be called play. Definitions of what counts as play are many and varied, generally revolving around the idea of purposive activities that do not appear to be directly goal oriented. "Goal orientation" is, of course, a problematic phrase. There is a fine body of research addressed to the topic of play versus work activities, but it doesn't appear to have had a deep effect on CSCW and its allied disciplines. From the standpoint of cultural criticism, the issue is not one of definitions of work or play, but of how the meanings of those terms are produced and maintained. Both work and play have culture-specific meanings and purposes, and I am conducting a quite culture-specific discussion when I talk about the primacy of play in human-computer interaction (HCI, or for our purposes just "interaction") as I do here.[5]

In order to clarify this point, let me mention that there are many definitions of interaction and many opinions about what interaction is for. As I write, large industry consortiums are finalizing their standards for what they call interactive multimedia platforms. These devices usually consist of a computer, color monitor, mouse, CD-ROM drive, sound card, and pair of speakers. This electronic instantiation of a particular definition freezes the conceptual framework of interaction in a form most suitable for commercial development—the user moves the cursor to the appropriate place and clicks the mouse, which causes something to happen—or what the interactivist Michael Naimark would call, more pejoratively, poke-and-see technology. This definition of interaction has been in the wind for so long now that few researchers say much about it. It is possible to play within the constraints of such a system, but the potential for *interaction* is limited, because the machine can only respond to an on-off situation: that is, to the click of the mouse. Computer games offer a few more input modes, usually in the form of a joystick, which has two or three degrees of freedom. However, from the standpoint of kind and gentle instruction, what the game companies do with this greater potential is not very inspiring. Technologically speaking, Sega's *Sewer Shark* (1993), for example, was an amazing exercise in game design for its time, but it reinforced the feeling that interaction in a commercial frame is still a medium like television, in which the most advanced product of the technological genius of an entire species conveys Geraldo Rivera to millions of homes in breathtaking color.

I don't want to make this a paradise-lost story, but the truth is that the definitions of interactivity used by the early researchers at MIT possessed a certain poignancy that seems to have become lost in the commercial translation. One of the best definitions was set forth by Andy Lippman, who described interaction as mutual and simultaneous activity on the part of both participants, usually working toward some goal—but, he added, not necessarily. Note that from the beginning of interaction research the idea of a common goal was already in question, and in that fact inheres interaction's vast ludic dimension.[6]

There are five corollaries to Lippman's definition. One is *mutual interruptibility*, which means that each participant must be able to interrupt the other, mutually and simultaneously. Interaction, therefore, implies conversation, a complex back-and-forth exchange, the goal of which may change as the conversation unfolds.

The second is *graceful degradation,* which means that unanswerable questions must be handled in a way that doesn't halt the conversation: "I'll come back to that in a minute," for example.

The third is *limited look-ahead,* which means that because both parties can be interrupted there is a limit to how much of the shape of the conversation can be anticipated by either party.

The fourth is *no-default,* which means that the conversation must not have a preplanned path; it must develop fully in the interaction.

The fifth, which applies more directly to immersive environments (in which the human participant is surrounded by the simulation of a world), is that the participants should have *the impression of an infinite database.* This principle means that an immersive interactional world should give the illusion of not being much more limiting in the choices it offers than an actual world would be. In a nonimmersive context, the machine should give the impression of having about as much knowledge of the world as you do, but not necessarily more. This limitation is intended to deal with the Spock phenomenon, in which more information is sometimes offered than is conversationally appropriate.

Thus interactivity implies two conscious agencies in conversation, playfully and spontaneously developing a mutual discourse, taking cues and suggestions from each other as they proceed.

In order to better draw this out let me briefly review the origins and uses of computers. Afterward I will return to the subject of play from a slightly different perspective.

The first devices that are usually called computers were built as part of a series of projects mandated by the military during World War II. For many years, computers were large and extremely costly. They were also cranky and prone to continual breakdown, which had to do with the primitive nature of their components. They required continual maintenance by highly skilled technicians. The factors of cost, unreliability, and the need for skilled and continual attention, not to mention the undeniable aura of power that surrounded the new machines like some heady smell, combined to keep computers available only to large corporations and government organizations. These entities came already equipped with their own ideas of efficiency, with the concepts of time and motion study then in vogue in industry (of which my colleagues have written at length), and of course with the cultural abstraction known as the work ethic perpetually running in the background. Even within the organizations themselves, access to the new machines was restricted to a technological elite which, though by no means monolithic in its view of technological achievement, had not had enough time to develop much of a sense, not to mention a sensibility, of the scope and potential of the new devices.

These factors combined to keep attention focused on the uses of computers as rather gross instrumentalities of human will—that is, as number crunchers and databases. Computers could extend human abilities, physically and conceptually. That is, computers were tools, like crowbars and screwdrivers, except that they primarily extended the mind rather than the muscles. Even Vannevar Bush's astonishingly prophetic "As We May Think" (1949) treated computers as a kind of superswitch. In this frame of understanding, computers were prosthetic in the specific sense of the Greek term *prosthenos*—extension. Computers assisted or augmented human intelligence and capabilities in much the same way that a machine or even another human being would; that is, as separate, discrete agencies or tools that occupied physical or conceptual spaces separate from those of the human.

It seems significant that the epistemic evolution that appeared to be gradually but inexorably making its way across Western cultures also manifested itself in a number of unexpected and quite unpredictable ways in cultural milieus far removed from the context of the Enlightenment and after. A pertinent though perhaps startling (and perhaps offensive) example is the aesthetics and philosophy of bullfighting. Prior to the schismatic work of the torero Juan Belmonte in the 1940s and '50s, the physical area in which bullfighting took place was divided into spaces of signification called "territories of the bull" and "territories of the torero." When designing his choreography for the bullring, Belmonte raised the heretical argument that since the human possessed the only agency in the arena, territory of the bull was a polite but fictional concept; all territories were territories of the torero. The choreographic movements Belmonte developed as a result of this argument transformed the character of bullfighting. The abstraction I call attention to here is the breakdown of boundaries between two systems of agency and how that transformation affects the play of power within a field of social action. In dance, Martha Graham articulated a similar revision of shared spaces of action, but somewhat closer to the center of what might be called traditional Western culture. Graham's relocating the center of agency to a hypothesized center of the body redefined the quality of contact that was possible between two agents. Susan Foster's theoretical and practical work on dance discusses these points in considerable detail.

All this changed in the 1960s, but the change was largely invisible both physically and conceptually. Deleuze and Guattari and Manuel De Landa and the eerie concept of the machinic phylum would not arrive on the scene for some 30 years. In 1962, the young hackers at Project MAC, deep in the bowels of MIT, made hardly a ripple in corporate arenas with their invention of a peculiarly engrossing computational diversion that they called *SpaceWar*.[7] This first computer game was still firmly identified with the military, even down to its name and playing style, but in that moment something quite new and (dare I say it) completely different had happened to the idea of computation. Still, it would not be until the 1970s that two kids in a garage in Mountain View, California, rather than a corporate giant like Sperry Rand or IBM or a government entity like the Bureau of Vital Statistics, would knock the props out from under the idea of computation-as-tool for all time.

Let me return to the discussion of work versus play once again, from the standpoint of computation and instrumentality. Viewing computers as calculatory devices that assist or mediate human work seems to be part of a Kuhnian paradigm that consists of two main elements. The first is a primary *human work ethic;* the second is a particularized view of *computers as tools*. The emergence of the work ethic has been the subject of innumerable essays, but the view of computers as tools has been so totally pervasive among those with the power to determine meaning in such forums as school policy and corporate ethics that only recently has the idea begun to be seriously challenged. The paradigm of computers as tools burst into existence, more or less, out of the allied victory in World War II (although the Nazis were working on their own computers). A paradigm of computers as something other than number crunchers does not have a similar launching platform, but the signs of such an imminent upheaval are perspicuous. Let me provide an example.

One of the most perceptive scholars currently studying the emergent computer societies is the anthropologist Barbara Joans. She describes the community of cyberspace workers as composed of two groups that she calls Creative Outlaw Visionaries and Law and Order Practitioners. One group has the visions; the other group knows how to build stuff and get it sold. One group fools around with technology and designs fantastic stuff; the other group gets things done and keeps the wheels turning. They talk to each other, if they talk to each other, across a vast conceptual gulf. These groups are invisible to each other, I think, because one is operating out of the older paradigm of computers as tools and the other out of the newer paradigm of computers as something else. Instead of carrying on an established work ethic, the beliefs and practices of the cultures I observe incorporate a *play* ethic—not to displace the corporate agendas that produce their paychecks, but to complexify them. This play ethic is manifest in many of the communities and situations I study. It is visible in the northern California Forth community, a group of radical programmers who have adopted for their own an unusual and controversial programming language; in the CommuniTree community, an early text-based virtual discussion group that adopted such mottos as "If you meet the electronic avatar on the road, laserblast Hir"; and in the Atari Research Lab, where a group of hackers created an artificial person who became real enough to become pro tem lab director. The people who play at these technosocial games do not do so out of any specific transformative agenda, but they have seized upon advantages afforded by differences of skill, education, and income to make space for play in the very belly of the monster that is the communication industry.

This production and insertion of a play ethic like a mutation into the corporate genome is a specifically situated activity, one that is only possible for workers of a certain type and at a certain job level. In specific, it is only possible to the communities who are perhaps best described as hackers—mostly young (although the demographic changes as the first- and second-generation hackers age), mostly educated (although the field is rife with exceptions, perhaps indicating the incapability of U.S. public schools to deal with talented individuals), mostly white (and exceptions are quite rare in the United States), and mostly male (although a truly egregious exception is part of this study). They create and use a broad variety of technological prosthetics to manifest a different view of the purpose of communication technology, and their continual and casual association with the cutting edge of that technology has molded them and their machines—separately and jointly—in novel and promising ways. In particular, because they are thoroughly accustomed to engaging in nontrivial social interactions through the use of their computers—social interactions in which they change and are changed, in which commitments are made, kept, and broken, in which they may engage in intellectual discussions, arguments, and even sex—they view computers not only as tools but also as *arenas for social experience.*

The result is a multiple view of the state of the art in communication technology. When addressing the question of what's new about networking, it's possible to give at least two answers. Let's stick with two for now.

Answer 1: Nothing   The tools of networking are essentially the same as they have been since the telephone, which was the first electronic network prosthesis. Computers are engines of calculation, and their

output is used for quantitative analysis. Inside the little box is information. I recently had a discussion with a colleague in which he maintained that there was nothing new about virtual reality. "When you
sit and read a book," he said, "you create characters and action in
your head. That's the same thing as VR, without all the electronics."
Missing the point, of course, but understandably.

Answer 2: Everything   Computers are arenas for social experience
and dramatic interaction, a type of media more like public theater,
and their output is used for qualitative interaction, dialogue, and conversation. Inside the little box are *other people*.

In order for this second answer to be true, we have to rethink some
assumptions about presence. Presence is currently a word that means
many different things to many different people. One meaning is the
sense that we are direct witnesses to something or that we ourselves
are being directly apprehended. This is what we might call the
straightforward meaning, the one used by many sober virtual reality
researchers. Another meaning is related to agency, to the proximity of
intentionality. The changes that the concept of presence is currently
undergoing are embedded in much larger shifts in cultural beliefs and
practices. These include repeated transgressions of the traditional
concept of the body's physical envelope and of the locus of human
agency. This phenomenon shows itself in such variegated forms as
the appearance and growth of the modern primitive movement, and
the astonishing fascination of a portion of the population with prosthetic implants. Simultaneously new companies spring up to develop
and manufacture wearable and eventually implantable computers.
The film *Tetsuo, the Ironman* appears, with its disturbingly florid
intermingling of biology and technology. William Gibson's cyberspace and Neal Stephenson's Metaverse are both science fiction in-
flections of inhabitable virtual worlds. A slow process of belief and
acceptance, perhaps most clearly instantiated in the process of cultural acclimatization to the telephone, accompanied by the issues of

warranting and authentication raised by the interjection into human social life of a technological object that acts as a channel or representative for absent human agencies.

In studying issues of presence, warranting, and agency, the work of theorists of dramatic interaction vis-à-vis computation, of which Brenda Laurel is an outstanding example, is invaluable. Many of the interesting debates involved in my research would not have been possible without the arguments Laurel presents in *Computers as Theatre* and elsewhere.

My first organized piece of research in the field of virtual systems involved studying a group of phone sex workers in the early 1980s. In this study I was doing two things. On one hand, I was beginning to develop some of the ideas I set forth here and, on the other, also discovering in microcosm the fascinating interplays between communication technology, the human body, and the uses of pleasure. If I were to frame some of the questions that occurred to me during that time, they might be these: How are bodies represented through technology? How is desire constructed through representation? What is the relationship of the body to self-awareness? What is the role of play in an emergent paradigm of human-computer interaction? And overall: What is happening to sociality and desire at the close of the mechanical age?

If I'm going to give in to the temptation to periodize—which I do again and again, though frequently with tongue in cheek—then I might as well take the period that follows the mechanical age and call it the virtual age. By the virtual age I don't mean the hype of virtual reality technology, which is certainly interesting enough in its own ways. Rather, I refer to the gradual change that has come over the relationship between sense of self and the body, and the relationship between individual and group, during a particular span of time. I characterize this relationship as virtual because the accustomed grounding of social interaction in the physical facticity of human bodies is changing. Partly this change seems good, and partly it seems bad. There are palpable advantages to the virtual mode in relation to the ways that the structure of cities and expectations of travel have changed with the advent of the telephone, the rise of large corporations, the invention and marketing of inexpensive tract housing, the development of the shopping mall, the commercial development and exploitation of electronic mass media, the development of the personal computer, the greening of large-scale information networks (which can be coopted for social interaction), and the increasing miniaturization of electronic components (eventually perhaps to be extended to mechanical devices, that is, Drexler and others). There are equally palpable disadvantages to each of these deep changes in our lives. I don't want this perhaps too-familiar list to be read as either extolling or condemnation. They are the manifestations, as well as causative agents, of the social changes, ruptures, and reorganizations that they accompany. In the course of this essay I sometimes organize the manifestation of these developments as a progressus, an ensemble of events that had a beginning and that leads in a particular direction. In doing so, I nod in the direction of Deleuze and Guattari, Paul Virilio, and Manuel De Landa.[8] But I am large; I contain multitudes. At other times the story is not at all meant to be teleological, because I don't foresee the telos toward which it tends. I may make some suggestions in that regard, but they are suggestions only and do not arise from any prophetic vision. I try to leave the prophetic side of things to my academic betters in the same line of work.

In the process of articulating the gradual unfolding of the cultural and technological foundations for virtual systems, I call on the work of scholars in a number of disciplines. One factor that bears importantly on the emergence of virtual systems is a change in the character of public space and the development and articulation of particular kinds of private space. I discuss this change in the context of portions of the social world of Elizabethan England with the help of the useful and important work of Francis Barker. In her study *The Tremulous Private Body,* Barker discusses from the point of view of textuality the creation of new social spaces; of particular relevance to our concerns here is a new and progressively ramified division of social space from a predominantly public space to a congeries of spaces increasingly privatized.[9] Barker uses the physicality of this new privatized space as a link to the metaphoricality of a symbolic and psychological private space that is both elicited by and is mutually supportive of its physical concomitant. In this regard the development of separate interior spaces within small dwellings—changes in philosophies of architecture and in methods of carpentry—is crucial.

The relationship of these changes to the changing concepts of interior and exterior space that enable and support the character of virtual systems is complex. In regard to the emergence of the concept of the interiorized cultural and epistemic individual, which we are by now used to calling the sovereign subject and to seeing as perhaps the most egregious product of the Enlightenment, this too bears a complex relationship to the changes in social and architectural space within which it is embedded. In his study *Segmented Worlds and Self,* Yi-Fu Tuan calls attention to these changes in the context of studies of architecture and subjectivity. Over time, Tuan shows, we can trace the emergence of an increasing social and epistemic privatization that leads to the idea of the individual, for better or worse, as we understand it today. The development of a palpable awareness of self can be followed through the changes by means of which it is produced, beginning in the Middle Ages when information first begins to accumulate—the increasing number of family and self-portraits; the increasing popularity of mirrors; the development of autobiographical elements in literature; the evolution of seating from benches to chairs; the concept of the child as a stage in development; the ramification of multiple rooms in small dwellings; the elaboration of a theater of interiority in drama and the arts; and most recently, psychoanalysis.

The development of a sense of individuality seems to be accompanied by a corresponding withdrawal of portions of a person's attention and energy from the public arena and their nourishment and concentration within the new arena of social action called the self. In the discourses with which we are perhaps most familiar, the self appears to be a constant, unchanging, the stable product of a moment in Western history. This seems a rather episcopal view of something that is not only better described as a process but that is also palpably in continual flux. Yet our institutions continue to be based on a fixed notion of what a self is—a local notion, a culturally delimited notion that inhabits the larger cultural infections of the mass media. It seems clear enough that the self continues to change, in fact has changed, beyond the snapshots we have of it that were taken within the last hundred years or so. The trends toward interiority and perhaps more importantly toward textuality that Barker reported still continue with increasing speed.

Further, they are abetted by concomitant developments in communication technology. Just as textual technologies—cheap paper, the typewriter, printing—accompanied new discourse networks and social formations, so electronic communication technologies—radio, television, computer networks—accompany the discourse networks and social formations now coming into being. These technologies, discourse networks, and social formations continue the trend toward increasing awareness of a sense of self; toward increasing physical isolation of individuals in Western and Western-influenced societies; and toward displacement of shared physical space, both public and private, by textuality and prosthetic communication—in brief, the constellation of events that define the close of the mechanical age and the unfolding or revealing of what, for lack of a better term, we might call the virtual age.

About Method

In regard to the term *virtual age,* I want it clear that when I talk about *ages, closes,* and *dawns,* it is not without being aware of what these words mean. I am grappling with the forms of historicization, and seeking—if frequently not finding—different ways to tell these stories. Pasted to one corner of my monitor screen I have a card that says,

No causes

No effects

Mutual emergence

which is also an extreme position. Death and furniture, as Malcolm Ashmore said: If somebody whacks me in the head, I could rightly attribute my headache to their intervention. Larger phenomena are, of course, tricky. I don't think I can show with any assurance what "caused" the Atari Lab, but I can tell a few of the stories that surround its coming into being, each one of which is situated in a web of stories of its own. If I could walk the walk as well as talk the talk, there would be no "ages" or "dawns" in this essay, and eventually, given time, I hope to produce a different account in which the events I discuss here are more deeply situated in their context . . . and vice versa.

My chosen method of representation for this attempt—a kind of adventure narrative interspersed with forays into theory—developed out of earlier work in which I mentioned that my hypothesized ideal method would be a cross between Sharon Traweek's *Beamtimes and Lifetimes* and Leo Tolstoy's *War and Peace*.[10] This piece/*peace* is a sally in that direction. It is thoroughly experimental and subject to recall for factory modification at any time. I feel that it is only through the process of trying out various forms of representation, some experimental and some not, that I can properly grapple with the formidable challenge of finding viable pathways into academic discourse in the time of cultural studies. ("In the time of . . ." There, I've done it again.)

Rather than presenting a succession of chapters explicating a common theme, I have tried to organize the work as a set of provocations whose central ideas remain more or less unstated—hovering, as I would like to imagine them, in the background. In this effort, my idealized stance as a novelist is the motivating concept. That is my *preferred, ideal* method; however, in the interests of avoiding some possibly unfortunate debates I have cheated and provided a theoretical section as well, and more explanation than I would have liked. I am still trying to move toward a methodology that Donna Haraway recently called cat's cradle. In other work I have mentioned that I prefer to thread these discourses and hold them in productive tension rather than allowing them to collapse into a univocal account, and cat's cradle describes this move perfectly. Haraway has added to my experimental statement the missing piece of community, of passing the accounts from hand to hand, perhaps turning them in different ways and threading them in new configurations, being ever mindful that we tell our stories within webs of power that distort them; and of course the important thing about a cat's cradle is that you can never let it collapse.

On Content

Although other accounts of cyberspace communities and the people who construct them are now appearing, it is possible that readers of this essay may not yet have encountered them; therefore, I include a few here. In any account of the advent of ludic interactive technology the MIT Media Lab occupies a central role as nurturer of almost all of the first generation of "reality hackers," and its founder, Nicholas Negroponte, continues to be seen as an individual with both tremendous foresight and stupendous abilities to attract capital and power.

When the first generation of young technokids left MIT in 1987 for the physical world (eschewing for now the slippery term *real*), many of them moved directly to a brand-new research lab financed by the Atari Corporation in California. The Atari Lab was headed by Alan Kay, who might have been compared to Negroponte in his ability to understand and navigate structures of power. It included among its staff the largest percentage of women in any laboratory up to that time and for a long time afterward, and this fact appears to have been due to Negroponte's influence both at the MIT Media Lab and on Alan Kay. The high attrition rates among women staff members that plagued most research labs did not affect the Media Lab in its early days. It appears that Negroponte's encouragement, his evenhandedness, and possibly his personal charm helped keep a cadre of bright young women in the lab long enough for Kay to hire them. Negroponte himself moved in a web of events that enabled and constrained his choices, including his secure and prestigious director-ship of *Le Grand Experiment*, the modestly named World Center for Research in Computation, just opened in Paris. The fortunes of the Atari Lab, unlike the Media Lab or the World Center, were tied to the continued success of a single company, and the glory days of Atari passed their peak shortly after its lab started work. But the days of success for both the Xerox Palo Alto Research Center and the World Center ended within a few months of the sudden fall of Atari, thus ending one of the most interesting and perhaps most promising pe-riods in prosthetic communication research.

A "golden window" of financial support, theoretical encourage-ment, free imagination, and peer camaraderie was open at Atari for perhaps two years, perhaps no longer than six months, depending upon which events seem important. But in that brief period the young researchers performed astonishing feats. The thrust of their work was toward issues of presence not in terms of an hypothecated "human-machine" interface, but in *situated* technologies that addressed such issues as gender and ethnicity. The impact of this work was largely lost on Atari, because of a hidden misunderstanding between Kay, the researchers, and Atari management about the purpose of the lab. This miscommunication didn't become visible until later, and conse-quently the young researchers' work remained to bear fruit at other research organizations at later times. When Warner sold Atari to the notorious Tramiel brothers, known in Silicon Valley for their blood-thirsty approach to entrepreneurism, the lab in its original form was doomed.[11] Its research group, composed of brilliant young men and an unusually high proportion of brilliant young women, suddenly found themselves on the street. As they scattered, they founded the first generation of companies directly associated with the develop-ment of what would come to be called virtual reality technology. The Atari Lab remains both emblematic of and the best example of a singular moment in the emergence of a constellation of ideas concerning what research in communication prosthetics and agency should be. The story of the Atari Lab makes up Chapter 6.

Already in California were several groups of computer engineers who saw computer technology as a transformative force for society. McLuhan-like, they believed that the technology itself was already producing deep changes in consciousness, but that belief would not stop them from hurrying things along. They developed programs to make dial-up bulletin boards into social forums within which certain people with access to computers and modems could quickly form new kinds of communities unrestricted by barriers of distance or, perhaps more significantly, of physical appearance. (They were not unrestricted by other means—such as ethnicity, class, income, and fluency in the English language.) Wide dissemination of the telephone numbers of these early virtual communities led to unexpected clashes as different and mutually incomprehensible cultures faced off within the electronic environment. As the survivors built new communities out of the ashes of the old, they unconsciously built much older Western theories of social life into their systems . . . such as defensive countermeasures, surveillance, and control. This might be called the Great Wall moment in the history of virtual systems, in retrospect a rather primitive beginning, but more sophisticated techniques were not long in arriving. The story of these events makes up Chapter 5.

Working in tandem with the early researchers were a few people who were directly concerned with designing and implementing environments for virtual social interaction. They designed their environments as games. The earliest of these were the multiple-user dungeons, or MUDs. The MUDs were direct descendants of a species of role-playing game known as Dungeons and Dragons, and they later changed (or rather attempted to change) the full name of their environments to multiple-user *domains* in an effort to attain a modicum of respectability.

The concept of MUDs was taken up as a research tool at the Xerox Corporation's Palo Alto Research Campus (PARC), where anthropologists have for a number of years observed social interactions within structured virtual environments with an eye toward eventual uses in the workplace. But the best known of the descendants of text-based MUDs was designed at LucasFilm as a pay-per-minute virtual game. Players entered *Habitat* via modem in the same way they would access any of the on-line services such as America Online or CompuServe. Once inside, they met other players, engaged in treasure hunts, apprehended (or became) criminals, published newspapers, married, divorced, and in general replicated in the virtual environment many of the pleasures and annoyances of life in the physical world. But the experiment never quite caught on in the United States. Almost unknown here, *Habitat* was acquired by Fujitsu, a Japanese company, and moved to a mainframe in Tokyo. There it became extremely successful, and attracted approximately 1.5 million inhabitants—an astonishing number even in light of LucasFilm's ambitious predictions for their American version.[12]

Habitat is a useful early example of how economies evolve in virtual spaces, in particular because sex work is a common form of employment in the simulation. Since Chip Morningstar and Randall Farmer had never thought of this eventuality when they wrote the code (they had no idea at all of what to expect of a graphic virtual environment), they didn't provide ways for inhabitants to assume any of the vanilla sexual positions. For example, there is no code to describe characters lying on top of each other, and a fortiori dog positions are unknown.[13] Thus in order to engage in sex in *Habitat* people must be inventive, and so they have been. Also, because Fujitsu keeps good records, it is possible to get some idea of how gender works in the space. An item of particular interest to me is that at any given time approximately 15 percent of the *Habitat* population is actively engaging in cross-dressing or crossgender behavior. After studying *Habitat* for a number of years I treat it only briefly here, in favor of a much longer account later in which I contrast it with newer graphic social environments. This account appears at the end of Chapter 5.

A subset of multiple-user domains consists of multiple-player games set in virtual environments. The earliest of these was a multiple-user environment called RBT, for Reality Built for Two, constructed at VPL Research in Palo Alto by one of the best-known of the first-generation virtual hackers, Jaron Lanier. Lanier's trademark dreadlocks became widely recognized in the world's business community when his picture (or more correctly, an engraving of his face—*WSJ* never uses photographs) appeared on the front page of the *Wall Street Journal* on January 23, 1990. Lanier's steamy hyperbole on the subject of virtual reality is legendary in the virtual communities, and if his entry into the world of international finance did not precisely signal the arrival of the young virtuality industry, at least it indicated that industry's vigor and sent a message that it should be taken seriously. In 1991, VPL was acquired by Thomson CSF. Thomson, which VPL modestly described in its investors' brochure as a "French electronics firm," is the largest defense contractor in Europe and was a major embarrassment to the largely Greenpeace-oriented VPL employees. Thomson's subsequent gutting of VPL in 1992 is by now well known.

Currently there is only one other player in the high-stakes field of virtual games entrepreneurship. That is John Waldern of W Industries, in Leicester, England. The informing philosophy behind W's games is the essential attraction of exotic total-immersion visual environments coupled with the proven thrill of bang-bang-shoot-'em-up action. While this use of the technology holds all the thrill for me of chopping up Abel Gance's *Napoleon* to insert commercials for TV viewing, there is no question that arcade games will represent a significant drive behind technological innovation in virtual-worlds equipment for the public sector. In addition, there also seems no question that a significant proportion of young people will spend a significant and increasing proportion of their waking hours playing computer-based games in one form or another, and so far the implications of this trend have yet to be fully addressed in academic forums. A major obstacle appears to be the feeling on the part of many academics that computer games are beneath serious notice, a situation perhaps best characterized as holding our cocktail party in a house that is already ablaze. Within a short time, the number of hours that a broad segment of children will spend playing computer-based games will exceed the number of hours that they spend watching television. It is entirely possible that computer-based games will turn out to be the major unacknowledged source of socialization *and* education in industrialized societies before the 1990s have run their course.[14]

While the current generation of multiple-player games would seem to have no particular redeeming virtue, their designers are among the fiercest of the techno entrepreneurs. In addition, of all the possible commercial uses bruited about for virtual-worlds equipment, multiple-player games are the only commercial application that is currently returning a profit. Clearly they speak to some deep desires on the part of a significant number of consumers. Thus there will inevitably be more of them.

It is impossible to study the emergence of virtual systems without acknowledging the overwhelming influence exerted upon the entire field of virtual technologies research by the military. The earliest large-scale virtual environments were built for military purposes by engineers who were working for military organizations: Ivan Sutherland, who began his research in three-dimensional displays in 1966, became director of the Information Processing Techniques Office at the Defense Advanced Research Projects Agency (DARPA); Tom Furness, who started the "Supercockpit" project for the U.S. Air Force in 1965, became chief of the Visual Display Systems Branch, Human Engineering Division of the Armstrong Aerospace Research Laboratory at Wright-Patterson Air Force Base; Scott Fisher and Mike McGreevy did a good deal of their work at NASA Ames in the late 1980s.

Sooner or later we can trace any funding back to government sources; if we include MIT, which has always been heavily funded by military budgets, there is almost no one working in the field today whose original research is not or was not funded by military money.

Still, some of the early and influential researchers were not directly involved with government funding. Myron Krueger is more of an artist than scientist; Jaron Lanier worked in the video game industry and wanted to become a composer; Fred Brooks is head of the computer science department at the University of North Carolina at Chapel Hill; Brenda Laurel took her M.F.A. at Ohio State in acting and directing, and later earned a Ph.D. in theater criticism. For better or worse, my focus in this essay is not on the military or even particularly on government; any number of my colleagues have done a far better and much more thorough job of studying military and government involvement in research and technological development than I could possibly do. In particular, Bruce Sterling's account of the U.S. military's networked environmental battle simulation SIMNET is eminently worth reading (although it may be hard to find, since it appeared in the now-scarce first issue of *Wired* magazine).

Several critical events in the development of virtual systems theory do not seem to me to fit comfortably into a narrative description of the emergence of the technology of virtual systems. The first documented account of a virtual cross-dresser, for example—a person who caused considerable consternation and some misery among the women in the virtual community that he frequented—requires a different sort of description from that accorded the first tree-structured bulletin board. It is difficult to look back over such a brief period to 1985 and realize how naive most inhabitants of the virtual communities were at the time "Julie Graham" was giving her sensitive and helpful, albeit unquestionably deceptive, advice to unhappy women on the nets. From the first documented instance to 1992, when at any given time 15 percent of the population of Habitat (or, by one estimate, 150,000 people) was engaged in crossgendered behavior, represents a span of seven years. A consideration of crossgendered behavior in virtual social spaces, in the form of an account of Julie's brief life and florid death, makes up Chapter 3.

The trial of a man who was accused of raping a woman with multiple personalities by seducing one of her personae is important to this work. The trial became something of a spectacle, recalling in new surroundings the old power to fascinate that still inheres in freaks and monsters, the power of near-legibility; it raised issues of multiplicity and continuity, of what constitutes a single identity in social and legal terms. The trial itself and the media circus that surrounded it were similar in useful ways to the landmark suit brought by the Mashpee Wampanoag Tribal Council, Inc., against the town of Mashpee, on Cape Cod, which James Clifford reported in his marvelous paper "Identity in Mashpee."

In his study Clifford identified three assumptions that he felt compromised the Mashpees' case against the government. He described these as (1) the idea of cultural wholeness and structure, (2) the hierarchical distinction between oral and literate forms of knowledge, and (3) the narrative continuity of history and identity. I found that Clifford's three points constituted a provocative background for the trial then under way in Oshkosh, Wisconsin, even in light of the fact that it was just such issues that the attorneys and judge in the Oshkosh case hoped would *not* intrude into an already complex debate.

I use the Oshkosh trial here to constitute a parallel narrative thread to my account of events in Silicon Valley in the 1970s and '80s, and as a specimen of one kind of public response to a visible transgression of cultural norms of unitary subjectivity. That is, it is not simply the spectacle of difference in operation, but a voice from the shadows— a reflection of deeper conflicts and negotiations regarding the physical and conscious expression of a drive for closure, which is one of Western culture's most important ways of making meaning. Joseph Campbell refers to the social emergence of the drive for closure as the *yoke of individuality*. There is nothing ontological about this idea. What I call the drive for closure is itself an emergent manifestation of the interactions of complex events and forces. At this point I become daunted by complexity. Maybe I'm talking about what Foucault calls power, and maybe not; whatever it is, it is damnably hard to describe. Samuel Delany once described power as something like a thin mist in a valley, which is all but invisible when one is in it, and which only becomes visible when one can look back on it from a height or a distance.[15] Delany said it in the context of a work of fiction, which is a mode of representation with which I have great sympathy; and how to say just that in an academic context is for me a serious preoccupation. At any rate I have chosen this account as emblematic and have placed it, along with a few others, in Chapter 2.

Development of self-awareness takes place in a field that is already contoured by that invisible and impalpable structure called power. And while there is still plenty of mystery about how the self manages to emerge under these circumstances, there is an even deeper mystery about how self and power mutually constitute each other. A particle physics approach to psychology: We see selves, and we see power, and we talk about how they exchange forces in terms of discrete quantities or thoroughly muzzy qualities; but at bottom there are still problems in representing this exchange in satisfying terms. Describing the sort of entities that could move easily through such a field and produce satisfying accounts is a concrete example of Haraway's Three Aspects of Representation, as discussed *passim* in her preface to *Coyote's Sisters* (Tokyo: Routledge, 1999).[16] For those who have not yet received their copies of *Coyote's Sisters,* of course the three aspects are these: Refuse closure; insist upon situation; and seek multiplicity.

In the concluding chapter I reconsider the disparate accounts I have presented and attempt to point out their correspondences and divergences *without* trying to produce an overarching theoretical framework that appears to encompass them all. In so doing I am performing the activity for which I was trained and which embroiled me in such mischegas in the Science Studies Program at San Diego: attempting to hold these various discourses in productive tension without allowing them to collapse into a univocal account. My game is for the reader—that's you—to perform your own synthesis, if synthesis is your game.

I treat the strategy I have just outlined as a challenge—the challenge of how to best convey information to an imagined "reader." This could come under a broader heading along with a constellation of issues generally identified as part of what is sometimes referred to as a crisis of representation in the social sciences. How best to convey a complex description of a culture whose chief activity is complex description? Here it is useful to keep in mind that while I am attempting to describe cultures of sorts, even though they do not fit many of the customary definitions of cultures,[17] it is necessary to embed other information that is equally important and that becomes something else if it is extracted from the context of cultural quasi-description.

The choice among the three or perhaps four representational methods that would best serve the purposes here would be quite difficult. If I had to narrow the field to two, the choice would be between the method that Ursula Le Guin employed with such excellent results in *Always Coming Home,* and I hope that her success with it will rub off on me in the future. The first part of the book would consist of parallel narrative threads interspersed with descriptions of artifacts, information on cultural byways, "tribal" songs and poetry, and some interpretation of "tribal" philosophy and epistemology by members of the "tribe." I would have left it at that but for what I feel are certain academic constraints, and consequently the second section would consist of my own theoretical interpretations of what is going on. The other possible choice, as I indicated earlier, would be a cross between Traweek's *Beamtimes and Lifetimes* and Tolstoy's *War and Peace.* Those who do not have much truck with anthropology of emergent or perhaps phantasmic cultures may find their purposes better served by ignoring these remarks.

Finally I do something that for lack of a better description might be called implications and consequences. Where does this stuff lead? What kind of world are these folks bringing into being? Or, perhaps to take up the questions raised by Deleuze, Guattari, and De Landa, what kind of system is using them to become realized? To address this question I frame my last few words in the context of a discussion with my daughter, who is eleven years old as of this writing and who is still trying to figure out just what it is that I do. And at the very end, my favorite person puts in an appearance—Anne Rice's fictional antihero the Vampire Lestat, who has mysteriously acquired a Ph.D. in anthropology. In the context of a work on cultural theory, Lestat may have a few pithy things to say about vision between the worlds.

1

Collective Structures

In the 1980s and early 1990s, in an extensive group of texts cutting across disciplines—including the military; big (and small) business; education; computer, social, and cognitive science; and psychology— it was perhaps the most quoted phrase of any new work of fiction: "A consensual hallucination experienced daily by billions. . . . Unthinkable complexity. Lines of light ranged in the nonspace of the mind, clusters and constellations of data. Like city lights, receding." These by-now-familiar lines are from William Gibson's (1984) description of cyberspace in his novel *Neuromancer,* the founding work for the genre of cyberpunk. Cyberspace is not just simulations, or military experimentation, or computer-supported work, but a space of pure communication, the free market of symbolic exchange—and, as it soon developed, of exotic sensuality mediated by exotic technology. The concept of cyberspace, which Gibson pulled from the kinds of electronic networking he saw already in use all around him, interpellated a large and diffuse assortment of workers in a variety of professional, academic, and military pursuits, as well as a considerable number of researchers whose work could not be collapsed into a traditionally identifiable category. They had been doing whatever they were doing for some time, but the arrival of *Neuromancer* was for many of them a signal announcing their existence to a larger audience, and simultaneously naming their subculture for themselves in a spectacular and definitive manner.

Since I began my research on cyberspace, Gibson's book, as well as those of the other early cyberpunk authors, has faded to backdrop, and cyberspace has gone from an interesting fantasy to a hotly contested financial, cultural, and ethical frontier. Some folks claim it has gone even further, on to ho-hum old business as usual. Newer works of what might be called (Goddess excuse me) postcyberpunk, such as Neal Stephenson's *Snow Crash,* have taken their turn at the leading edge of popular culture.

What was so sizzling about the whole thing? Cyberspace as Gibson described it was a physically inhabitable, electronically generated alternate reality. It was entered by means of direct links to the brain; that is, it was inhabited by refigured human "persons" separated from their physical bodies which were parked in "normal" space. In cyberspace, the physical laws of "normal" space did not need to apply, although some experiential rules carried over from normal space; for example, the geometry of cyberspace as Gibson described it was Cartesian. In *Neuromancer* the "original" body was the authenticating source for the refigured person in cyberspace; no "persons" existed whose presence was not warranted by the concomitant existence of a physical body back in "normal" space. But death in either normal space or cyberspace was real, in the sense that if the "person" in cyberspace died, the body in normal space died also, and vice versa.

In later novels in the Neuromancer series, Gibson allowed his concept of cyberspace to evolve. Among other things, he gave up the idea that consciousness in cyberspace had to be warranted in a physical body. This change had interesting consequences, for example, the appearance in cyberspace of orishas and loas, as well as hints of "oversoul" structures that did not manifest as bounded entities.[1] It also helped to both mollify and enflame (take your pick) the hordes of literary critics, cultural theorists, computer scientists, feminist theorists, hackers, and religious fundamentalists who had jumped into the cyberspace fray with gusto and enthusiasm.

As Gibson maintained from the beginning, to a certain extent cyberspace does exist now, as a metaphor for late-twentieth-century communications technologies, for instance, as data banks, financial systems, computer networks, military simulations, and ATMs. As John Perry Barlow, the Grateful Dead songwriter who is also a founder of the Electronic Frontier Foundation, says: When you put your card into your automated teller, cyberspace is where your money is. For the rest of Gibson's vision—the dizzying world of the console cowboy—of course, many of us live at least part-time in cyberspace already. We call it computer conferencing, or phone sex, or virtual this or that, but insofar as it involves communicating with other people through narrow-bandwidth media, it is about negotiating the tensions between individual subjects, virtual collectivities, and the physical bodies in which they may or may not be grounded. Although Gibson's cyberspace arrived with the publication of a particular text in 1984, it crystallized certain debates surrounding meaning in connection with particular technological and cultural objects that had themselves been in existence for some time. Thus the cultural ascension of the term *cyberspace* had both positive and negative results. The positive side is perhaps ubiquitous, at least if one is a hacker, but the negative side concerns how cultural debates over beliefs and practices in communications technologies that might have crystallized in different forms were dragged into the cyberspace definition by its immense conceptual/gravitational field. Thus all of the elements of virtuality have come to possess a greater or less association with the idea of cyberspace, including those that do not particularly relate to it. They have all been with us for many years in various forms—visually as dioramas and botanical gardens, aurally as radio dramas, kinesthetically as carnival rides, textually perhaps as novels.

The network of electronic communication prosthetics for which cyberspace is the metaphor has achieved visibility in the context of late capitalism, in the historical moment of biosociality (Paul Rabinow's term for the collapse of the distinctions between biological observation, construction, and control, as in the Human Genome Project) or technosociality (my term, in playful juxtaposition to

Rabinow's and referring to the state in which technology and nature are the same thing, as when one inhabits a network as a social environment). I am interested in cyberspace for a number of reasons. First, because it is a social environment. The networks are elsewheres where we can observe new collective structures risking themselves in novel conditions. These structures take the form of organized and moderated conferences, multiuser groups, anarchic chats, clandestine assignations. Some are trivial, some are definitely not trivial and have real effects outside the nets. Some of the interactions are racially differentiated and gendered, stereotypical and Cartesian, reifying old power differentials whose workings are familiar and whose effects are well understood. But some of the interactions are novel, strange, perhaps transformative, and certainly disruptive of many traditional attempts at categorization.

Second, I am interested in cyberspace because the kinds of interactions we can observe within the spaces of prosthetic communication are for me emblematic of the current state of complex interaction between humans and machines. Third, the identities that emerge from these interactions—fragmented, complex, diffracted through the lenses of technology, culture, and new technocultural formations—seem to me to be, for better or worse, more visible as the critters we ourselves are in process of becoming, here at the close of the mechanical age. I see these identities engaged in a wonderful and awesome struggle, straining to make meaning and to make sense out of the very idea of culture as they know it, swimming for their lives in the powerful currents of high technology, power structures, and market forces beyond their imagination. In this struggle I find certain older structures stubbornly trying to reassert themselves in a technosocial milieu that to them seems to have gone berserk. These are the structures of individual caring, love, and perhaps most poignant, of desire.

While there is an obvious retrogressive danger in posing these cultural formations and collective structures as being in opposition, and thereby of reifying in my analysis the whole ontology of binarism which so much of cultural theory—including my own—attempts to reframe and deconstruct, I am at heart a novelist . . . a shameless teller of stories. That's why titling this book *The War of Desire and Technology at the Close of the Mechanical Age* is something I do with considerably mixed emotions, but, in fine, have chosen to do. Mindful of the ontic danger signals implicit in the words *war, close,* and *age,* I still find myself—like my favorite antihero, Anne Rice's Vampire Lestat—doing it anyway. And, as we will see later, Lestat himself plays a larger role in this cultural transformation than we might suppose.

The War of Desire and Technology is about science fiction, in the sense that it is about emergent technologies, shifting boundaries between the living and the nonliving, optional embodiments . . . in other words, about the everyday world as cyborg habitat. But it is only partly about cyberspace. It is also about social systems that arise in phantasmatic spaces enabled by and constituted through communication technologies. To some extent they exist in the cultural milieu suggested by Gibson's cyberspace metaphor. But they also considerably predate *Neuromancer.* Their existence both validates Gibson's dark and dystopic vision, points beyond it to other, perhaps more congenial visions, and also shows how the cyberspace metaphor emerged from cultural processes long under way.

I am not a neutral observer. I live a good part of my life in cyberspace, surfing the nets, frequently feeling like a fast-forward flaneur. I am interested in prosthetic communication for what it shows of the "real" world that might otherwise go unnoticed. And I am interested because of the potential of cyberspace for emergent behavior, for new social forms that arise in a circumstance in which *body, meet, place,* and even *space* mean something quite different from our accustomed understanding. I want to see how tenacious these new social forms are in the face of adversity, and what we can learn from them about social problems outside the worlds of the nets. I want to see how groups of friends evolve when their meeting room exists in a purely symbolic space. I want to see how narrowing the bandwidth—that is, doing without customary modes of symbolic exchange such as gesture and voice tone—affects sharing and trust, and how inhabitants of virtual systems construct and maintain categories such as gender and race. I want to see how people without bodies make love.[2]

The predominant mode of these emergent forms is what I have called the technosocial, in playful appreciation of Paul Rabinow's theory of the biosocial. Rabinow describes biosociality as the gradual implosion of the categories of nature and culture, exemplified in research into genetics as an extension of structures of civilization over areas formerly considered "natural." Rabinow says that "in biosociality, nature will be modeled on culture understood as practice; it will be known and remade through technique; nature will finally become artificial, just as culture becomes natural. . . . The objectivism of social factors is now giving way to . . . the beginnings of a redefinition and eventual operationalization of nature."[3] When I look for new social forms in cyberspace, it is with this process in mind. I am seeking social structures in circumstances in which the technological is the natural, in which social space is computer code, consensual and hallucinatory.

This trek into the mysterious recesses of technology, which in the case of computer technology is ultimately the binary, in search of the natural is reminiscent of some classical tropes with which we may be familiar. Of course there is an ironic twist to this Conradesque search: I am suggesting a venture not into the heart of "nature" in search of redemption but rather into the heart of "technology" in search of nature. And not nature as object, place, or originary situation, but rather in Haraway's sense nature as Coyote, the Native American trickster-spirit animal—that is, as diversity, flexibility, irruption, playfulness, or put briefly, nature as *actant,* as process, continual reinvention and encounter, that actively resists, disrupts—in sum (in Haraway's words), queers—representation. When I speak of life in the nets as technosocial, I am pointing to what both Rabinow and Haraway imply, with a hopeful eye on the future not of technology but of the social forms within technology-viewed-as-nature—those social forms to whom technology has become invisible, in no more and no less the same way that the workings of our bodies have become invisible in the face of a burgeoning medical imaging industry whose premise is to make the body thoroughly visible—social beings for whom technology *is* nature, for whom elsewhere *is* geography, for whom the problematic tie between unitary awareness and unitary physical body has *political* consequences. I want to see if cyberspace is a base camp for some kinds of cyborgs, from which they might stage a coup on the rest of "reality."

Over the past few years I have written a number of articles about political entities viewed as fixed in place by a hypertrophy of location technologies. The purpose of location technology is to halt or reverse the gradual and pervasive disappearance of the socially and legally constituted individual in a society in which the meanings of terms such as *distance* and *direction* are subject to increasing slippage. And this slippage, of course, does not refer only to the physical or geographic, but to the other, non-Cartesian modes of location. Freud was perhaps the first to perform a kind of codification upon this imaginal territory, in that he produced a detailed and, it was believed, replicable body of knowledge that was concerned with the territory of the unconscious—a territory which, of course, was invented and culturally produced in the act of definition. However, it was not Freud's articulation of the unconscious that concerns us here, but rather the production of diagnostic criteria which accompanied Freud's work—the seeds of what is now called the *DSM,* the *Diagnostic and Statistical Manual of Mental Disorders,* published by the American Psychiatric Association. The *DSM* is an example of the kinds of location technologies to which I refer, because in the process of defining a psychological disorder it simultaneously produces, organizes, and legitimizes a discursive space that has quasi-Cartesian concomitants. The inhabitant proper to this space is the virtual entity of psychological testing, census taking, legal documentation, telephone numbers, street addresses—in brief, a collection of virtual elements that, taken together, form a *materialized discursivity* of their own that I refer to as the fiduciary subject.[4] I have found this idea a useful way to articulate the (always political) tie between what society defines as a single physical body and a single awareness of self.

Thus the technology that produces and maintains the fiduciary subject not only produces a discursive landscape, but simultaneously calls into being inhabitants of that landscape who are proper to its geography and character. Such a landscape and such inhabitants might be a trivial exercise; after all, an almost equivalent definition would work for the discursive landscape of the theater or television. The link to its importance, however, is precisely that . . . namely, a link, a coupling between the phantasmic space that the location technology calls into being and the physical space of pain and pleasure that the human body inhabits. This critical element differentiates what is important from what is trivial in virtual space. I refer to the production and maintenance of this link between a discursive space and a physical space as warranting. By means of the process of warranting, for example, the political apparatus of government is able to guarantee the production of what would be called a citizen. Broadly, this citizen is composed of two major elements. One is the collection of physical and performative attributes that Judith Butler and Kobena Mercer in separate works call the culturally intelligible body.[5] The other is the collection of virtual attributes which, taken together, compose a structure of meaning and intention for the first part. Taken together, these two broadly defined elements compose a socially apprehensible citizen.

I want to be careful in making these distinctions that I do not reify dichotomies already in place. There is always a danger in distinguishing the body from some other collection of attributes linked to the body. I want to be quite clear that the physical/virtual distinction is *not* a mind/body distinction. The concept of mind is not part of virtual systems theory, and the virtual component of the socially apprehensible citizen is not a disembodied thinking thing, but rather a different way of conceptualizing a *relationship* to the human body. In this sense virtual systems theory is rather like epistemological feng shui, the Chinese art of placement. With this in mind, let me carry the discussion further.

The socially apprehensible citizen, then, consists of a collection of both physical and discursive elements. Although the physical elements possess a special and bounded order of reality on account of their particular relationship to the social disciplines of pain and pleasure, the remainder of the citizen—by far the greater part, the part which is also concerned with the production of meaning of the physical part—is discursive. By means of warranting, this discursive entity is tied to an association with a particular physical body, and the two together, the physical and the discursive, constitute the socially apprehensible citizen. Within a political framework, the discursive entity—including the meaning associated with the physical body—is produced by means of texts, such as legal, medical, and psychological description. Because so much of such an identity is discursive and is produced through the actions of texts, I have elsewhere referred to it as *legible* body, that is, as textually mediated physicality. The legible body is the social, rather than physical, body; the legible body displays the social meaning of "body" on its surface, presenting a set of cultural codes that organize the ways the body is apprehended and that determine the range of socially appropriate responses.

To my knowledge, William Gibson was the first writer to deal with the issue of warranting. Although he did not specifically refer to the phenomenon, it is implicit in his understanding of the ontology of cyberspace. In *Neuromancer,* a death in cyberspace meant that the physical body in biological space also died—that is, that there is an implied link between the virtual body (or more properly the discursive convergences that constitute and maintain the discursive body in cyberspace), and the convergences of discourses, some of which are of similar nature to the virtual, that constitute the body in physical space—a link which is powerful enough to carry information that the physical (i.e., biological) body interprets or understands as physical (e.g., sickness and death). A rough and inexact analogue to this link is the phenomenon referred to as virtuality sickness, a sensation of nausea which is caused by the time lag between a physical head movement and the concomitant change in viewpoint or perspective within a virtual simulation. Virtuality sickness is far from death, although it is unpleasant, but it demonstrates the principle to which I refer.

The role of the human sciences in articulating the discursive moves that produce the fiduciary subject has been discussed at length in other contexts by, for example, Foucault. In *The History of Madness*, Foucault discusses the epistemological and social moves by means of which certain people are excluded from normal social intercourse. The result of these moves is the discursive space that simultaneously organizes and calls into being the rational social order. Later, in *The Birth of the Prison*, Foucault describes a method of dividing and organizing physical space so as to make the inhabitants of that space available for observation; this process is accomplished in ways that presage the gradual transformation of the citizen into streams of information, a process that Haraway identifies as part of the production of the cyborg.[6]

In contrast to the relentlessly monistic articulations of physical and virtual space that law and science favor, let us juxtapose the mode of the technosocial, of reinvention and encounter in a technological space viewed as itself a social and physical environment, as a kind of nature. In the idealized view of such a space, the very elements that Foucault saw as being suppressed in the process of "gridding" reassert themselves in novel ways—irruptively constituting identities that are simultaneously technological and social, a catastrophic emergence of the ludic and the unpredictable at the very heart of the ordered mathematical structures that by their nature seek to suppress it. This process is possible, in fact inevitable, because the technosocial, the social mode of the computer nets, evokes unruly multiplicity as an integral part of social identity. There is plenty of precedent for multiplicity as a response to violence, and certainly enough for multiplicity as a response to less overt methods of subjection; in fact, in a pun on Klausewitz's remark that war is politics by other means, it is tempting to describe multiplicity as resistance by other means—keeping in mind that multiplicity alone, of which we have ample evidence, does not in and of itself constitute a *successful* resistance (it is important not to forget the danger of simple responses, of what Leila Cosu-Lughod has called the romance of resistance), but it is still a response that is perspicuous in incidences of psychological abuse and stress.

Some forms of multiple personality are useful examples of such a social mode ready to hand. Further, in the language of the programmers who already inhabit the frontiers of the technosocial, multiple personality is a mode that is already in place, fairly debugged in the current release. Multiples exist around us here and now, and regardless of the bad press accorded to multiple personality "disorder," some remain invisible, living their lives quietly and gracefully. Their situation suggests many of the issues of passing and "outing" that are familiar from other discourses.

I do not want to suggest that there is some magical or redemptive quality to multiple personality, but rather that the way in which multiplicity plays itself out within a physical and psychological frame is highly suggestive of a broader abstraction of human behavior, one that is particularly noticeable in the technosocial framework of virtual systems. The multiple is the enantiomorph, the opposite, of the unitary monistic identity that location technology produces. The multiple is the socializer within the computer networks, a being warranted to, but outside of, a single physical body. The body in question sits at a computer terminal somewhere, but the locus of sociality that would in an older dispensation be associated with this body goes on in a space which is quite irrelevant to it.

The cyborg, the multiple personality, the technosocial subject, Gibson's cyberspace cowboy all suggest a radical rewriting, in the technosocial space (which is largely constituted by textual production, much of which is the computer code by whose prosthetic mediation a significant portion of the space of technosociality exists), of the bounded individual as the standard social unit and validated social actant. For example, the well-known multiple Truddi Chase, according to her psychologist/author, consists of 92 supposed "functions." In her study of multiple personality and trauma, "The Horror of No Longer Remembering the Reason for Forgetting," Thyrza Goodeve points out:

> Truddi's troops (who, for the most part, significantly, do not go by conventional "names," but by what we might call "functions"—*The Interpreter, The Gate Keeper, The Buffer, The Recorder,* for example)—explain their origin as "an intellectual reproduction system."[7] The individual, imploding under the pressures of her material conditions, disappears, and the emergent construction, developing from the ashes of violence, seems something much closer to the population of a "small town," or an ever flickering series of switching television channels—but never that embattled Cartesian *cogito* so often presumed by the pronoun "I."[8]

Such fractured identities call attention to alternatives, always multiple, always in tension. Just as changes in complex "real-world" political economies presage a radical simplification of biological diversity, the ramification of complex social systems in the *alter* space of communications technologies suggests a war between simplification and multiplicity . . . an explosion of actors and actants that includes the almost-living, the not-living, and the never-living, arising in the boundaries between technology, society, and "nature," in the architectures of multiple embodiments and multiple selves. We already have a considerable industry built around its promise, although we never refer to it in those terms. There is, of course, nothing fortuitous about these developments. Never has so much attention been paid to, so much big money spent on, a phenomenon that originated as science fiction only ten years earlier. A look at the origins of virtual systems may suggest that the effort is driven by more than either defense needs or market forces can explain.

2

Risking Themselves: Identity in Oshkosh

From an article in the *San Francisco Chronicle:*

On July 23, 1990, a 27-year-old woman filed a complaint in Oshkosh, Wisconsin charging that Mark Peterson, an acquaintance, raped her in her car. The woman had been previously diagnosed as having Multiple Personality Disorder (MPD). She claimed that Peterson raped her after deliberately drawing out one of her personalities, a naive young woman who he thought would be willing to have sex with him.

Cut to: the municipal building complex in Oshkosh, Wisconsin.[1] Outside the courthouse, gleaming white media vans lined the street, nose to tail like a pod of refrigerators in rut. A forest of bristling antennas reached skyward, and teenagers in brightly colored fast-food livery came and went bearing boxes and bags; the local pizza joints were doing a land-office business keeping the crews supplied. The sun was very bright, and we blinked as we emerged from the shadows of the courthouse. "Jim Clifford would have loved this," I commented. "I wonder what the Mashpee courthouse looked like during the trial he was researching."

"Where's Mashpee?" my friend asked.

"In New England. The town of Mashpee was originally an Indian village. The Mashpee Indians deeded some land to the settlers, and the settlers eventually took over everything. A few years ago the surviving Mashpee families sued the town of Mashpee to get their land back, claiming that it had been taken from them illegally. When the suit finally came to trial, the government argued that the case revolved around the issue of whether the Mashpee now were the same Mashpee as the Mashpee then. In other words, were these Mashpee direct descendants of the original Mashpee in an uninterrupted progression.

"So the issue really being argued was, just what in hell is cultural continuity, anyway? Is it bloodline, like the government wanted it to be, or is it the transmission of shared symbols and values, like the view that the Mashpee themselves seemed to hold?

"That's why I find this trial so interesting, because what they're arguing here is almost the identical thing. Except instead of what is a culture, the thing running in the background is what is a person. We all say, 'I'm not the person I was then,' but to not only the government but also everybody else, that's a figure of speech."

While we stood in line there were a million and one other things I wanted to add. For example, the idea that personal identity is so refractory is a culturally specific one. Changing your name to signify an important change in your life was common in many North American cultures. Names themselves weren't codified as personal descriptors until the Domesday Book. The idea behind taking a name appropriate to one's current circumstance was that identity is not static. Rather, the concept of one's public and private self, separately or together, changes with age and experience (as do the definitions of the categories *public* and *private*); and the name or the label or the identity package is an expression of that concept. The child is mother to the adult, but the adult is not merely the child a bit later in time.

Retaining the same name throughout life is part of an evolving strategy of producing particular kinds of subjects. In order to stabilize a name in such a way that it becomes a permanent descriptor, its function must either be split off from the self, or else the self must acquire a species of obduracy and permanence to match that of the name. In this manner a permanent name facilitates control; enhances interchangeability . . . if you can't have a *symbolic* identity (name) that coincides with your actual state at the time, then your institutionally maintained or *fiduciary* identity speaks you; you become the generic identity that the institutional descriptors allow.

On this particular day, the first day of what by anybody's definition could be called the spectacle of multiplicity, everyone was getting 15 seconds of fame, each person's own little niche in the spectacle, as multiplicity and violence were processed through the great engine of commodification just like everything else. Reporters from media all over the world were interviewing everything that moved. There were only so many people available in Oshkosh, and after exhausting whatever possibilities presented themselves in the broad vicinity of the municipal complex, the media began to devour each other in a typical paparazzi feeding frenzy. On the lawn not far from the courthouse doors Mark Blitstein, a reporter for the *Oshkosh Herald*, a small local newspaper, was grinning broadly. "I was just interviewed by the BBC," he said.

The cult of Isis reached full flower in Egypt around 300 B.C.E., in the New Kingdom during the Persian Dynasties. The consul Lucius Cornelius Sulla brought the Isis myth to Rome in 86 B.C.E., where it took root and flourished for nearly 700 years, becoming for a time one of the most popular branches of Roman mythology. The last Egyptian temples to Isis were closed sometime in 500–600 C.E.

The outlines of this familiar myth are simple: At first there existed only the ocean. On the surface of the ocean appeared an egg, from which Ra, the sun, was born. Ra gave birth to two sons, Shu and Geb, and two daughters, Tefnut and Nut. Geb and Nut had two suns, Set and Osiris, and two daughters, Isis and Nephthys. Osiris married his sister Isis and succeeded Ra as king of the earth. However, his brother Set hated him. Set killed Osiris, cut him into pieces, and scattered the fragments over the entire Nile valley. Isis gathered up the fragments, embalmed them, and resurrected Osiris as king of the netherworld, or the land of the dead. Isis and Osiris had a son, Horus, who defeated Set in battle and became king of the earth.

In his foundational work in abnormal psychology, *Multiple*

Personality Disorder (1986), Colin Ross makes the point that the
Isis/Osiris myth illustrates the fragmentation, death, healing, and resurrection of the self in a new form. He probably chose this as his
representative morphotype because it is more widely familiar than
many other versions of what Joseph Campbell called the resurrection
mythoid, an iconic fragment of human belief systems which Campbell
asserted recurs across cultural boundaries. (Campbell had other
problems with his theory that need not concern us here. We would
be more likely to look to structuralism for similar theoretical
approaches.)

   Ross used the Osiris myth as a specific therapeutic model. He maintained that the MPD patient suffered from an Osiris complex, rather
than an Oedipus complex. His abandonment of the Oedipus complex
as a useful explanatory model stems from his reading of Freud's interpretation of the case of Anna O. and Freud's repudiation of the seduction theory following the publication of *Studies in Hysteria*. Ross's
rationale is partly one of explanatory economy; he points out that
the Oedipal model is what hackers would call a kluge—a complex,
unwieldy, and aesthetically unsatisfactory patch that has the singular
virtue of getting the job done—and that the Osiris model (not to
mention the accompanying Isis model that would replace the Elektra
complex) provides a much simpler and more elegant explanatory
framework for multiple personality.

   There were certainly enough varied opinions about what in hell
was going on here to supply a very large number of theoreticians.
The knots of professionals of various stripes engaged in muted or
heated discussions called to mind the gedankenexperiment of setting
an infinite number of monkeys to the task of writing the complete
works of Shakespeare. Harold Wasserman, one of the psychologists
observing the trial, commented, "There's an awful excess of attention
being paid to MPD these days. You know, in many ways it's being
grossly overdiagnosed. And people are being channeled into it . . .
it's like your most recent designer disease."

"What else is it good for?"

"It's also a way to get attention because of its fashionability in some therapeutic circles. There's no doubt that Sarah is a person who is not well. But she's learned to channel her illness so it gets attention. Or maybe so she gets attention. But that way of dealing with a psychological problem has its own difficulties. It's also self-damaging. Part of her way of expressing it is to burn herself with cigarettes. Then her other personalities wonder how she got burned."

"Is there a possibility that she was acting? To get attention, I mean."

Wasserman shook his head, looking thoughtful. "If she was acting, it was a hell of a brilliant job. And if she wasn't acting, then there was something else going on that was quite fascinating. Her vocabulary and demeanor, for instance . . . over time and place, they're consistent within a personality."

"How can you be sure that a particular person really has MPD and isn't faking it for some reason?"

"In many cases it's terribly hard to say . . . very difficult to make the call. Most MPDs are very intelligent. I'd think the more intelligent you were, the better you'd be able to fake something like that. If you were mentally ill anyway and knew it, there'd be excellent reasons to get a designer disease. You might be worried about getting lost in the state hospital system, and coming up with symptoms of MPD is a hell of a good way to get lots of attention really fast. If I were committed to a state facility, you bet I'd generate a good case of MPD just as fast as I possibly could. That kind of thing can easily make the difference between life and death in some places, or between a reasonably comfortable life and being zombified by compulsory meds 24 hours a day."

"I'm not really sure just what this stuff is, how it works, or really anything as simple as reliable diagnostic procedures. A good part of what we're seeing here is a very tight interaction between the patients and the doctors, where a certain amount of this stuff is occurring in the interactions between them, and that makes it very difficult to tell what's really going on. Do you get MPD when you're diagnosed or when you're two years old? I'd like to find out, but it gets more difficult every day. The thing is taking on a life of its own.

"But in this case, at least, there's not much argument about whether the incident between Sarah and Mark Peterson really happened . . . that's not what's at stake. After all, Sarah's condition wasn't exactly a secret. Her friends knew; the neighbors knew she had MPD. And Peterson . . . Jesus." He shook his head. "It was clear to everybody that the guy was a real sleazebag, and that he was lying . . . after all, he bragged about it afterward to friends. Hell, he bragged about it to the *cops*."

Rather than delegating the trial to a prosecutor, Winnebago County District Attorney Joseph Paulus handled the case himself. He took Peterson through the hoops, then doubled back. "Let's get back to your making love to Jennifer," Paulus said.

Peterson immediately corrected him. "I never said I made love to her."

Paulus looked faintly annoyed, went back to his table, and riffled through a pile of papers there. "We have a statement here from you, in which . . . ah"—he found the page he was looking for—"you gave Officer Barnes a statement in which you claimed to have made love to Jennifer."

"Well, I . . . that's not right."

"Would you like me to read it to you?" Paulus was looking at the papers in his hand; he barely looked up when he said it.

"No. I mean I know what I said, and that statement was incorrect."

Paulus's eyebrows came up a trifle, but his expression didn't change. "In your statement to Officer Barnes you said that you and Sarah had discussed her multiple personalities before you went to the park, is that correct?"

"No, sir."

"You didn't talk about her multiple personalities with her?"

"No, sir."

"At any time?"

"That's right."

Paulus put most of the papers down, or rather slapped them down, and rounded on Peterson. He was plainly angry. "You allowed all kinds of untruths to go into this statement, didn't you?"

Peterson fumbled for a moment. "I was tired from a long day's work," he said.

Freud and Breuer published their classic work *Studies in Hysteria* in 1895. The book consisted of some case histories of their female patients and a number of chapters on theory. All the women described in the case histories had what would be theoretically described as dissociative disorders. In addition, most had been sexually abused. In Ross's view, Anna O., the subject of the most famous case history in the book, "clearly had MPD." Up to that point, Freud had considered these patients as suffering from the adult consequences of real childhood sexual abuse. His treatment took the reality of the trauma into account from both clinical and theoretical perspectives.

However, within a few years of publishing *Studies in Hysteria*, Freud repudiated the seduction theory which he had so carefully and effectively worked out. This point in Freud's development of his psychoanalytic theory has been a focus for study for some time; for example, Ernest Jones pointed out in his 1953 biography of Freud that many of the abusive fathers of Freud's dissociative female patients were part of Freud's social circle. This fact would have made it extremely awkward for Freud to state publicly that his patients had been sexually abused as children. Anna O.'s family lived in the Liechtensteinerstrasse, only one block from the Bergasse, where Freud both lived and worked. Breuer, for his part, was extremely uncomfortable with the sexual aspects of Anna O.'s symptomatology (Jones 1953, 247).

Edward Salzsieder, Peterson's attorney, started out with a novel and, until that moment, an unthinkable idea. Salzsieder suggested that even though Wisconsin law forbade questioning a rape victim about her sexual history, such protection shouldn't extend to all of her other personalities. So he proposed questioning the other personalities—Franny and Ginger in particular—about *their* sexual histories. Many observers felt that this was one of the key points in the definition of multiple personality as a condition or state with legal standing other than as a pathology. For better or worse, Judge Hawley didn't think much of the idea. He did appreciate its complexity, though—"We're trying to split some very fine hairs here," he said— but he wasn't willing to take the idea so far as to impute autonomy to the multiples. "I do find," he said, "that the rape shield law applies to [Sarah] and all her personalities combined."

That threw Salzsieder back on his own resources. Deprived of the opportunity to question the personalities about their individual sexual exploits, he fell back on the strategy of attacking their legitimacy. To bring this off he needed to assemble a cadre of MPD infidels, unbelievers with legal and professional stature who, he hoped, could cast doubt on the whole idea of MPD. As it turned out, it wasn't difficult to do. All kinds of people were willing to testify on all sides of the issue. But Salzsieder was looking for a special person, someone who not only didn't believe in MPD but also could convince a court that MPD was a convenient fantasy, something that Sarah had read about and then adopted to excuse her promiscuous behavior. Eventually he came up with Andrew Powell. Powell is from Pennsylvania, a slightly balding man of medium build who when on the stand projects the proper blend of sober professionalism and easy believability that Salzsieder needed. Powell is an impressive infidel. He is an articulate speaker who is convinced that MPD is a medical hoax. Salzsieder had gotten him to review Sarah's psychiatric records for the previous year.

Salzsieder started by getting Powell to attack the credibility of MPD as a diagnostic category. After Powell was sworn in, Salzsieder asked, "How many psychologists actually have patients with MPD?"

"There's a band of very intense believers who have all the sightings, where the rest of us never see any," Powell said. "What I call the UFOs of psychiatry."

"In your professional opinion, what would you call Sarah's condition?"

Powell put his fingertips together like a character from a Perry Mason episode. "I would say that . . . I believe Sarah does have psychiatric problems, but her problems don't appear grave enough to fit within the *DSM3* guidelines."

"She's well enough to know what she's doing. Is that what you mean? Responsible for her own actions?"

"That's correct."

In his foundational account of MPD, Colin Ross identifies the fragmentation of self and the transformation of identity that occur across ethnic and cultural boundaries, all of which he lumps together under the rubric of "aberration." While his identification of this characteristic of human cultures is correct, his use of the rubric is peculiarly situated. Ross is interested in making a strong case for legitimizing MPD as a recognized medical phenomenon, and in so doing he seems to feel that he must explain away the problem of why many of the cultures he mentions in passing do not themselves pathologize MPD. Ross can perhaps be excused for pathologizing MPD *tout court*, because he evinces a genuine interest in assisting the individuals he has observed whose accommodation to buried trauma causes, in his words, more suffering than it prevents. I am primarily concerned here with how the phenomenon of multiple personality fits into a broader framework of cultural developments in which the abstract machine of multiplicity (in Deleuze and Guattari's words) is grinding finer and finer. Among the phenomena at the close of the mechanical age that it is useful to note is the pervasive burgeoning of the ontic and epistemic qualities of multiplicity in all their forms.

It was the moment everyone in the courtroom had been waiting for. People had been standing in line since before dawn to assure themselves of seats in the courtroom. A few had brought folding chairs to use while they waited in the predawn chill. Some sat on beach blankets with thermos jugs of steaming coffee. The composition of the crowd was extraordinarily diverse.

After an agonizing wait while people chatted to each other with the same lively animation that I associated with waiting for the start of a long-anticipated film, the bailiff called the room to order. The silence was instantaneous. "All rise," the bailiff called, and Judge Hawley strode in, followed by the court stenographer.

Hawley sat down in the high-backed leather chair, squared something on his desk, and looked down from the bench at the packed courtroom, his glasses catching the light. The sound of people getting seated died away, and a hush again fell over the room.

For the most part Hawley had not said very much beyond what was required of him as presiding magistrate, but this morning he cleared his throat and made a brief introductory speech. His voice carried well in the room. It was a calm voice, not too inflected.

"Before we proceed any further, I want to make sure all the video and film equipment in this room is turned off and that all the cameras are down out of sight." He scanned the room slowly, more for effect than for surveillance, then continued in the same calm voice. "There has been an unusual amount of attention surrounding this case. The issues we are considering are of an unusual nature. But I want to make it clear to everyone here that this is not a circus. This is a very sensitive case. There may be some bizarre behavior that you have not witnessed before. But nothing should get in the way of this being a court of law, first and foremost. I know that I can expect you to behave appropriately."

Nods from the spectators. People settled deeper into their seats. The unusually large population of professionals among the spectators now made itself known as people reached into bags and briefcases for their yellow notepads, making the room bloom like a gray field dotted with buttercups.

Hawley nodded to Paulus. The silence deepened, if that were possible, and Paulus called his first witness of the day.

Sarah walked briskly to the stand. She seated herself and was sworn in. She put her hands in her lap and looked calmly at Paulus. This is the main event, I thought. It is what this whole thing is about, really. It is not columns in a newspaper. It is not theory or discussion. It is not sound-bite media hype. It is a young, calm, slightly Asian-looking woman in a short-sleeved white cotton sweater and a calf-length pale blue skirt.

Paulus stood a few feet in front of her, holding his body relaxed and still. He spoke to her in a normal conversational tone, not very loud but clearly audible in the silent room.

"Sarah, you've heard some testimony here about some events that took place recently in Shiner Park. Do you recall that testimony?"

Sarah nodded slightly, then added, "I do."

"Do you have any personal knowledge as to the events in the park?"

"No," Sarah said, "I do not." Her voice was quiet, flat, matter-of-fact.

"Who would be in the best position to talk about the events in the park that night?"

"Franny," Sarah said.

"Would it be possible for us to, uh"—Paulus hesitated and looked like he wanted to clear his throat, but he settled for an instant's pause instead and then continued—"meet Franny, and talk to her?"

"Yes," Sarah said, looking calmly at him. A beat or two. "Now?"

"Yes," Paulus said. "Take your time."

The silence was absolute. Faintly, from somewhere outside in the hallway, something metallic dropped to the floor and rolled.

Sarah closed her eyes and slowly lowered her head until her chin was resting on her chest. She sat that way, her body still, breathing slowly and shallowly. It seemed as though everyone in the room held a collective breath. The muted hush of the air conditioning came slowly up from the background as if someone had turned up a volume control.

Maybe five seconds passed, maybe ten. It felt like hours. Then she raised her head, and slowly opened her eyes.

She looked at Paulus, and suddenly her face was animated, alive, and mobile in a way that it hadn't been a moment before. The muscles around her mouth and eyes seemed to work differently, to be somehow more robust. She looked him up and down, taking him in with obvious appreciation. "Hel-*lo*," she said.

"Franny?" Paulus said, inquisitively.

"Good morning," Franny said. She looked around at the windowless courtroom. "Or good afternoon—which is it?" Her phrasing was more musical than it had been, with an odd lilt to the words. It, too, was animated, but it didn't sound quite like an animated voice should have sounded. Also, on closer inspection it appeared that the more animated look of her features hadn't made it down into her body. Her posture, the way she held herself, the positions of her shoulders and legs and the relative tension in the muscles of her body, hadn't changed very much from Sarah's posture.

Paulus looked as if he wanted to feel relieved, but again he hid it quickly. "It's, uh, morning, actually," he said, in a conversational tone. "How are you today?"

"I'm fine. How are you?" The same lilt to the words.

"Just fine. Now I was just talking to Sarah a few moments ago, and I'd like to talk to you about what happened June ninth of 1990." He glanced up at Hawley. "But before we do that, the judge has to talk to you."

Hawley looked down at Franny. When she faced forward most of what he could see of her was the top of her head, but she turned now to face him. Her expression was hard to catch, but Hawley looked perfectly placid, as if swearing in several people in one body were something he did every day. "Franny," he said, "I'd like you to raise your right hand for me, please."

Hawley swore her in, his face impassive. It sounded like any other court ritual. When they got to the "so help you God" part, Franny said, "Yes," they both lowered their hands, and she turned back to Paulus.

"What did he say?"

"He said it felt good. And I knew what I was supposed to do when he said that. I seen it on TV. People wiggling like that. And when a person says it feels good, the other person is supposed to say it feels good. So I put my arms around his back, and I said, 'That feels nice.' "

"Did it feel nice?" Paulus asked.

"No," she said, sounding perplexed. "But you're supposed to say that, aren't you? It was on TV."

An important aspect of Freud's personal genius, and one with lasting import for the developing field of psychoanalysis, was his ability to construct a clinically plausible and *socially acceptable* theory that explained the phenomena of adult dissociation and simultaneously denied the reality of childhood sexual abuse. This, which Ross refers to as Freud's unfortunate "metapsychological digression," was the theory of the Oedipus and Elektra complexes. Returning resolutely to his point, Ross asserts that the Osiris complex more clearly describes what happens in the etiology of MPD than the Oedipus or Elektra complex can, and it does so with a minimum of description; if economy of representation counts for anything, the Osiris complex wins hands down. The trouble with the Osiris myth in a modern clinical frame, as Ross comments, is that, "in our culture, the original agent of the fragmentation of self does not always receive divine retribution."

From the point at which Freud repudiated the seduction theory, and continuing forward almost to the present, psychoanalysts of Freudian persuasion considered patients with dissociative disorders of traumatic origin to be suffering from unresolved unconscious incestuous fantasies. This state of affairs has been treated at length by feminist scholars (e.g., Rivera 1987, 1988; Sprengnether 1985; etc.).

We are still looking at traumatically produced MPD here, still using the final D to indicate that the thing is a disorder and nothing more. Just what is it, then, that we are looking at, and why is MPD so important to an examination of communication technology? More to the point, is there any room for nontraumatic multiplicity in any of these clinical accounts? At one point Ross, for example, answers this question almost dismissively and with complete self-confidence: "The term [multiple personality] suggests that it is necessary to debate whether one person can really have more than one personality, or, put more extremely, whether there can really be more than one person in a single body. Of course there can't" (Ross 1986, 41). And here Ross misses some of the most crucial implications of his study.

Multiple personality (without the stigmatizing final D) is a mode that resonates throughout the accounts I present here. Ross's research both affirms and denies that mode in a complex way. He has a clear investment in affirming the reality of a clinical definition of multiplicity, and his views concerning Freud's problems in coming to grips with the probable etiology of clinical multiplicity (with the D) are useful in studying the influence Freud has had on the field of psychoanalysis. For reasons that I find not entirely clear, he dismisses out of hand the idea that there can be more than one person in a single body. At that point he appears to fall back on received social and cultural norms concerning the meaning of "person" and "body." Like the surgeons at the Stanford Gender Dysphoria Project, of whom I have written elsewhere,[2] Ross still acts as a gatekeeper for meaning within a larger cultural frame, and in so doing his stakes and investments become clearer.

In this context, the context of multiplicity and psychology, it is useful to consider the work of Sherry Turkle. In her study "Constructions and Reconstructions of the Self in Virtual Reality," presented at the Third International Conference on Cyberspace, Turkle notes:

The power of the (virtual) medium as a material for the projection of aspects of both conscious and unconscious aspects of the self suggests an analogy between multiple-user domains (MUDs) and psychotherapeutic milieus. . . . MUDs are a context for constructions and reconstructions of identity; they are also a context for reflecting on old notions of identity itself. Through contemporary psychoanalytic theory which stresses the decentered subject and through the fragmented selves presented by patients (and most dramatically the increasing numbers of patients who present with multiple personality) psychology confronts the ways in which any unitary notion of identity is problematic and illusory. What is the self when it functions as a society? What is the self when it divides its labor among its constituent "alters" or "avatars"? Those burdened by post-traumatic dissociative syndrome (MPD) suffer the question; inhabitants of MUDs play with it.

In Turkle's context, the context of virtual systems, the question that Ross dismisses as, to him, obviously false—namely, can multiple selves inhabit a single body—is irrelevant. It is irrelevant because the socioepistemic structures by means of which the meanings of the terms *self* and *body* are produced operate differently in virtual space. Turkle not only perceives this difference acutely, but seizes upon it and turns it into a psychotherapeutic tool. Moreover, Turkle shows how the uses of virtual space as an adjunct to therapy translate across domains, beyond the virtual worlds and into the biological. What in this context might be called the ultimate experiment—plugging a person with MPD into the MUDs—has yet to be performed. Thus we have not yet observed one of its possibly hopeful outcomes: healing trauma, but preserving multiplicity; or perhaps more pertinent, creating discursive space for a possibly transformative legitimization of some forms of multiplicity. The answers to the questions posed previously—why is MPD so important to an examination of communication technology, and is there room for nontraumatic multiplicity in clinical accounts—in fine are bound up with the prosthetic character of virtuality. The technosocial space of virtual systems, with its irruptive ludic quality and its potential for experimentation and emergence, is a domain of nontraumatic multiplicity. Turkle and others, myself included, are waiting to observe how the dialogue between nontraumatic multiplicity and clinical accounts emerges in a new therapeutic context.

"Do you remember what you talked about while he was there?"
"Most of it was small talk. I recall telling him that we were many, there were many of us in the body. I said we were multiple, that we shared the body. I told him about some of the others."
"How did he react to your telling him about some of the others?"
"He didn't seem surprised."

Although everyone had his or her own reason for being there, observers could not quite explain their fascination with the courtroom scene. I tried to make a few mental models, but the attempt didn't work. The courtroom audience's behavior, though, was its own giveaway. Their attention was on the moment of rupture, conjoining the sacred and the forbidden. I am certainly not the first to label this moment the moment of interruption, when the seamless surface of reality is ripped aside to reveal the nuts and bolts by which the structure is maintained. Sarah was a liminal creature, marked as representing something deeply desired and deeply feared. In the same court an ax murderer would attract a certain ghoulish attention, but nothing like the fascination we were seeing here. On the principle that where one finds a circumstance which is a focus of the most intense emotional energy coupled with the least understanding of why it is such a focus, there is the place to dig, then it seemed clear enough that the moment Franny appeared was that moment.

The spectacle, I think, is not unlike Foucault's descriptions of public executions.[3] Multiple personality, as it is commonly represented, is the site of a massive exercise of power and of its aftermath, the site of a marshaling of physical proof that identity—of whatever form—arises in crisis. It vividly demonstrates the connection between the violence of splitting off a string of identities to the violence of representation under the sign of the patristic Word in a court of law. In order for the prosecution's strategy to work, the victim must manifest a collection of identities each one of which is recognizable to the jury as a legal subject. In our view of this spectacle, we find ourselves constituted in a particular position as viewers in the same way that Foucault describes the viewer's position in his disquisition on Velázquez. We are witnesses to an exercise of power, to a fixing in position of a particular subjectivity. Having thus been drawn to the grotesque—in this case, to the spectacle of the maimed persona—we might reflect on how we got here and where we were going when our attention was arrested.

First is the spectacle of violence at the margins, at the origins of subject construction. To make the discredited move from the local to the universal, in the violence by which the multiple subject is constituted in the medical syndrome we recognize the elements by which national identities have traditionally arisen—the consolidation of a sense of conscious autonomy in an act of violence, temporally and physically at the site of its application. We are witnesses to a spectacle that as civilized beings we would prefer not to acknowledge—a site at which the apparatus of production of subjectivity is laid bare— and consequently we cannot bring ourselves to name it. Instead we view it as an aberration, as pathology, engendered by an unfortunate encounter with a sick author(ity). We fail to make the identification when confronted with a particular narrative of passage, that of recognizing the protagonist as oneself. We miss the lesson of how we came to be capable of being constructed as witnesses *ab origine,* miss comprehending our own violent origin.

The trial ends with Peterson's conviction.

This outcome is a mixed grill for the various interests surrounding the trial. While there are several points on which new law might have been written, two in particular are interesting in connection with the Peterson trial. One concerns the conflation of multiple personality with mental illness. Another concerns the legal status of each member of a multiple personality. Both of these relate to issues of how cultural meaning is constructed in relation to bodies and selves.

Ruth Reeves, Sarah's downstairs neighbor, had no particular investment in much of the debate. "I've met most of them [the personalities], and they're real," she said. "It's no different, really, than talking to a roomful of people."

"Do you think she's sick . . . mentally ill? I mean, multiple personality as a disease . . ."

"Well, her personalities mostly just seem to live their lives. It's not like one of them's a murderer or goes around busting up the furniture. Some of them aren't healthy for her, though. I hope therapy can help her, so she doesn't have to do things like eat crayons or burn herself. But—" She looked thoughtful for a moment, searching for words.

"You know," she said, "if the therapy turns out to be effective I'm going to *miss* the personalities. They're a wonderful bunch of folks."

The verdict upholds existing Wisconsin law. The law states that it is a crime to have sex with a mentally ill person who is so severely impaired that he or she cannot appreciate the consequences of the behavior, and if the other person knows of the illness. Because the trial made no attempt to separate the issue of MPD from issues of mental illness, the verdict reinforces the general conflation of multiple personality with mental illness. This outcome seems natural to the great majority of mental health professionals who viewed the trial. A few, who perceived the opportunity to "decriminalize" MPD, are disappointed.

Multiple personality covers a broad range of phenomena, which includes within its spectrum such things as spirit possession. *Multiple personality disorder* is the official term for a condition that includes, among other things, blackouts. That is, only one personality is out at a time, and if there is a dominant personality it suffers memory gaps during the time the other personalities are out. "You find clothes in your closets that you have no memory of having bought, and worse yet, they aren't the cut or color you would ever think of buying," one multiple says. "You get court summonses about traffic violations you didn't commit, you wake up in the morning and find you have burns and bruises and you have no idea how or where you got them." In general the dominant personality is frightened and troubled by these occurrences. The dominant personality may also have difficulty coping in the world, and it is this maladjustment, or the fear and disorientation caused by the blackouts, that generally brings the person into the doctor's office.

At the other end of the spectrum are persons who also consider themselves multiples but do not suffer blackouts and claim to retain awareness of what the alter personalities are doing when they are out. These persons find themselves in a difficult situation. If they assert their multiplicity, they fear being pathologized, so they tend to live "in the closet," like other marginalized groups. They live largely clandestine existences, holding regular day jobs and occasionally socializing with other multiples of similar type. They worry about being discovered and being forced to quit their jobs, or about being declared disabled or mentally incompetent. They have no common literature that unites them; the multiple equivalent of Radclyffe Hall's *Well of Loneliness* has yet to be written. Their accustomed mode of existence, sharing a single body with several quasi-independent personalities, is emblematic of a fair percentage of everyday life in the world of virtual systems.

3

In Novel Conditions:
The Cross-Dressing Psychiatrist

Underlying the story of multiplicity and continuity as it unfolded in Oshkosh is a tangle of multiply nested assumptions. One thread of this tangle is that one of our Western industrialized cultural assumptions is that subjectivity is invariably constituted in relation to a physical substrate—that social beings, people, exist by virtue of possessing biological bodies through which their existence is warranted in the body politic. Another is that we know unproblematically what "body" is. Let me tell you a boundary story, a tale of the nets, as a means of anchoring one corner of the system of discourse within which this discussion operates. It is also a fable of loss of innocence—which, I have begun to notice, is the tenor of more than one story here. In the course of this essay a number of chapters partake of the loss-of-innocence motif . . . in retrospect, a surprising number. People who still believe that I have some sort of rosy vision of the future of virtual systems are advised to reread a few of the origin myths I present in these pages. Herewith, another.[1]

This one begins in 1982, on the CompuServe conference system. CompuServe is owned by Reader's Digest and Ziff-Davis. CompuServe began in 1980 as a generalized information service, offering such things as plane reservations, weather reports, and the "Electronic Shopping Mall," which is simply lists of retail items that can be purchased through CompuServe and ordered on-line. It was one of perhaps three major information services that started up within a year or so of each other. The others were The Source, Prodigy, and

America Online. All of these were early attempts by businesses to capture some of the potential market formed by consumers with computers and modems, an attempt to generate business of a kind that had not previously existed. None of the on-line services knew what this market was or where it lay, but their thinking, as evidenced by reports in the *Wall Street Journal,* was along the lines of television. That is, computers would be media in which goods could be sold visually, like a shopping service. Prodigy implemented this theory by having banners advertising products running along the bottom of the screen, while permitting conferencing to go on in the main screen area. The companies who financed The Source seem to have believed that unrestricted conversation was against the American Way, because it was never permitted to occur within the system. Both Prodigy and The Source saw their primary mission as selling goods. They attracted audiences in the same way that broadcasters did, as a product to be delivered to manufacturers in the form of demographic groups meant to watch commercials. The Source went quietly bankrupt in 1986. Prodigy, by virtue of having permitted on-line conferencing, weathered the storms of the shakeout days in which it became clear that whatever on-line services were good for, it was *not* to deliver audiences to manufacturers. CompuServe, however, found out quite early that the thing users found most interesting was on-line conferencing and chat—that is, connectivity. Or, as an industry observer put it, "People are willing to pay money just to connect. Just for the opportunity to communicate." America Online never saw itself as a medium for selling goods and concentrated on connectivity in various forms from the beginning.

Most on-line conferences now offer what are called chat lines, which are virtual places where many people can interact simultaneously in real time. In the Internet world there are many such places with quite elaborately worked out geographies; these are known as multiple-user thisses-and-thats.[2] The first of these were direct descendants of real-life things called role-playing games, or RPGs.

Role-playing games were developed within a rather small community whose members shared certain social traits. First, most were members of the Society for Creative Anachronism, or SCA, one of the driving forces behind the Renaissance Faires. The SCA sponsors medieval tournaments with full regalia as well as medieval banquets in medieval style, which is to say, 16-course meals of staggering richness. Once one has attended such a banquet, the shorter life span of people in the Middle Ages becomes much more understandable.

Participants are extremely dedicated to the principles of the SCA, one of which is that tournaments go on as scheduled, rain or shine. In California, where many SCA members live, this can be risky. There is something not exactly bracing about watching two grown men in full armor trying to whack each other with wooden swords while thrashing and wallowing through ankle-deep mud and pouring rain. During this phase of my research I got a glimpse of what it must be like to be trained as a traditional anthropologist, and finally to be sent to some godforsaken island where one thrashes out one's fieldwork in a soggy sleeping bag while being wracked by disabling parasites and continuous dysentery.

Second, many of the people who belong to the SCA also consider themselves part of what is sometimes called the neopagan movement. And third, particularly in California, many of the people who participate in SCA events and who belong to the neopagan movement are also computer programmers.

Originally RPGs seemed to be a way for SCA members to continue their fantasy roles between tournaments. Role-playing games are also a good deal less expensive and more energy efficient than tournaments. They have tremendous grab for their participants, are open-ended, and improve with the players' imaginations. Some RPG participants have kept a good game going for years, meeting monthly for several days at a time to play the game, eating, sleeping, and defecating in role. For some, the game has considerably more appeal than reality. They express an unalloyed nostalgia for a time when roles were clearly defined, folks lived closer to nature, life was simpler, magic was afoot, and adventure was still possible. They are aware, to a certain extent, that their Arthurian vision of the Middle Ages is thoroughly bogus, but they have no intention of allowing reality to temper their enthusiasm.

The first RPG was published as a set of rules and character descriptions in 1972 and was called, appropriately enough, Dungeons and Dragons. It was an extension, really, of SCA into a textual world. D&D, as it quickly became known, used a set of rules invented by the Austin game designer Steve Jackson called the Generic Universal Role Playing System, or GURPS, for constructing characters, and voluminous books containing lists of character attributes, weapons, and powers. A designated Dungeon Master acted as arbiter of disputes and prognosticator of events and had considerable effect on the progress of the game; creative Dungeon Masters, like good tops, were hard to find and, once discovered, were highly prized.

The first 120- and 300-baud modems became available in the mid-1970s, and virtually the instant that they became available, the programmers among the D&D community began to develop versions of the game that could be played on-line. The first on-line systems ran on small personal computers (the very first were developed for Apple II's). Because of the problems of writing multitasking operating systems, which allow several people to log in on-line at once, the first systems were time-aliased; that is, only one person could be on-line at a time, so simultaneous real-time interaction was impossible. The first of these to achieve a kind of success was a program in northern California called *Mines of Moria*. The program contained most of the elements that are still ubiquitous in on-line RPG systems: Quests, Fearsome Monsters, Treasure, Wizards, Twisty Mazes, Vast Castles, and, because the systems were written by young heterosexual males, the occasional Damsel in Distress.[3]

As the Internet came into being from its earlier and more cloistered incarnation as ARPANET, more people had access to multitasking systems. The ARPANET had been built around multitasking systems such as Bell Laboratories' UNIX and had packet-switching protocols built in; these enabled multiple users to log in from widely separated locations. The first on-line multiple-user social environments were written in the early 1980s and were named, after their origins, Multiple-User Dungeons or MUDs. When the staid academics and military career persons who actually oversaw the operation of the large systems began to notice the MUDs in the mid-1980s, they took offense at such cavalier misuse of their equipment. The writers of the MUDs then tried the bald public-relations move of renaming their systems Multiple-User *Domains* in an effort to distance themselves from the offensive odor of play that accompanied the word *dungeon*. The system administrators were unimpressed by this move. Later multiple-user social environments came to be called MUSEs (for Multiple-User Social Environment), MUSHes (for Multiple-User Social Host), MUCKs, and MOOs (MUD Object-Oriented). Of these, all are somewhat similar except for the MOO, which uses a different and much more flexible method of creating objects within the simulation. Unlike MUDs, objects and attributes in a MOO are persistent; when the MOO crashes, everything is still in place when it comes back up. This property has importance for large systems such as Fujitsu's *Habitat* and smaller ones that contain many complex objects, such as the MIT Media Lab's MediaMOO and the U.Texas ACTLab's PointMOOt.

The multiple-user social environments written for the large, corporate-owned, for-pay systems betray none of their origins in low culture. They do not contain objects, nor can objects be constructed within them. They are thoroughly sanitized, consisting merely of bare spaces within which interactions can take place. They are the Motel 6 of virtual systems. Such an environment is the CB chat line on CompuServe. It was on CompuServe, some time early in 1982, that a New York psychiatrist named Sanford Lewin opened an account.

In the conversation channels, particularly the real-time chat conferences such as CB, it is customary to choose an on-line name, or "handle," that may have no relationship to one's "real" name, which CompuServe does not reveal.[4] Frequently, however, participants in virtual conversations choose handles that express some part of their personalities, real or imagined. Lewin, with his profession in mind, chose the handle "Doctor."

It does not appear to have dawned on him that the term was gender-neutral until a day not long after he first signed on. He had been involved in a general chat in public virtual space, had started an interesting conversation with a woman, and they had decided to drop into private mode for a few minutes. In private mode two people who have chosen to converse can only "hear" each other, and the rest of the people in the vicinity cannot "hear" them. The private conversation was actually under way for a few minutes before Lewin realized it was profoundly different from any conversation he'd been in before. Somehow the woman to whom he was talking had mistaken him for a *woman* psychiatrist. He had always felt that even in his most personal conversations with women there was always something missing, some essential connection. Suddenly he understood why, because the conversation he was now having was deeper and more open than anything he'd experienced. "I was stunned," he said later, "at the conversational mode. I hadn't known that women talked among themselves that way. There was so much more vulnerability, so much more depth and complexity. And then I thought to myself, Here's a terrific opportunity to help people, by catching them when their normal defenses are down and they're more able to hear what they need to hear."

Lewin reasoned, or claimed to have reasoned, that if women were willing to let down their conversational barriers with other women in the chat system, then as a psychiatrist he could use the chat system to do good. The obvious strategy of continuing to use the gender-neutral "Doctor" handle didn't seem like the right approach. It appears that he became deeply intrigued with the idea of interacting with women *as a woman,* rather than using a female persona as a masquerade. He wanted to become a female persona to such an extent that he could feel what it was like to be a woman in some deep and essential way. And at this point his idea of helping women by becoming an on-line woman psychiatrist took a different turn.

He opened a second account with CompuServe under the name Julie Graham.[5] He spent considerable time working out Julie's persona. He needed someone who would be fully functioning on-line, but largely unavailable off-line in order to keep her real identity secret. For the most part, he developed an elaborate and complex history for Julie, but creating imaginary personae was not something with which he had extensive experience. So there were a few minor inconsistencies in Julie's history from time to time; and it was these that provided the initial clues that eventually tipped off a few people on the net that something was wrong. As it turned out, though, Julie's major problems didn't arise from the inconsistencies in her history, but rather from the consistencies—from the picture-book life Lewin had developed for her.

Julie first signed on in 1982. She described herself as a New York neuropsychologist who, within the last few years, had been involved in a serious automobile accident caused by a drunken driver. Her boyfriend had been killed, and she had suffered severe neurological damage to her head and spine, in particular to Broca's area, which controls speech. She was now mute and paraplegic. In addition, her face had been severely disfigured, to the extent that plastic surgery was unable to restore her appearance. Consequently she never saw anyone in person. She had become a recluse, embittered, slowly withdrawing from life, and seriously planning suicide, when a friend gave her a small computer and modem and she discovered CompuServe.

After being tentatively on-line for a while, her personality began to flourish. She began to talk about how her life was changing, and how interacting with other women in the net was helping her reconsider her situation. She stopped thinking of suicide and began planning her life. Although she lived alone and currently held no job, she had a small income from an inheritance; her family had made a fortune in a mercantile business, so at least she was assured of a certain level of physical comfort. She was an atheist, who enjoyed attacking organized religion; smoked dope, and was occasionally quite stoned on-line late at night; and was bisexual, from time to time coming on to the men and women with whom she talked. In fact, as time went on, she became flamboyantly sexual. Eventually she was encouraging many of her friends to engage in net sex with her.

Some time during this period Julie changed her handle, or sign-on pseudonym, as a celebration of her return to an active social life, at least on the net. She still maintained her personal privacy, insisting that she was too ashamed of her disfigurements and her inability to vocalize, preferring to be known only by her on-line persona. People on the chat system held occasional parties at which those who lived in reasonable geographic proximity would gather to exchange a few socialities in biological mode, and Julie assiduously avoided these. Instead she ramped up her social profile on the net even further. Her standard greeting was a huge, expansive "HI!!!!!!!!!!!"

Julie started a women's discussion group on CompuServe. She also had long talks with women outside the group, and her advice was extremely helpful to many of them. Over the course of time several women confided to her that they were depressed and thinking about suicide, and she shared her own thoughts about her brush with suicide and helped them to move on to more life-affirming attitudes. She also helped several women with drug and chemical dependencies. An older woman confided her desire to return to college and her fear of being rejected; Julie encouraged her to go through with the application process. Once the woman was accepted, Julie advised her on the writing of several papers (including one on MPD) and in general acted as wise counsel and supportive sister.

She also took it upon herself to ferret out pretenders in the chat system, in particular men who masqueraded as women. As Van Gelder pointed out in her study of the incident, Julie was not shy about warning women about the dangers of letting one's guard down on the net. "Remember to be careful," Van Gelder quotes her as saying, "Things may not be as they seem."[6]

There is a subtext here, which has to do with what I have been calling the on-line persona. Of course we all change personae all the time, to suit the social occasion, although with on-line personae the act is more purposeful. Nevertheless, the societal imperative with which we have been raised is that there is one primary persona, or "true identity," and that in the off-line world—the "real world"—this persona is firmly attached to a single physical body, by which our existence as a social being is authorized and in which it is grounded. The origin of this "correct" relationship between body and persona seems to have been contemporaneous with the Enlightenment, the same cultural moment that gave birth to what we like to call the sovereign subject. True, there is no shortage of examples extending far back in time of a sense of something in the body other than just meat. Usually this has to do with an impalpable soul or a similar manifestation—some agency that carries with it the seat of consciousness, and that normally may be decoupled from the body only after death. For many people, though, the soul or some impalpable avatar routinely journeys free of the body, and a certain amount of energy is routinely expended in managing the results of its travels. Partly the Western idea that the body and the subject are inseparable is a worthy exercise in wish fulfillment—an attempt to explain why ego-centered subjectivity terminates with the substrate *and* to enforce the termination. Recently we find in science fiction quite a number of attempts to refigure this relationship, notably in the work of authors like John Varley, who has made serious tries at constructing phenomenologies of the self (e.g., Varley 1986).

Julie worked off her fury at drunk drivers by volunteering to ride along in police patrol cars. Because of her experience at neuropsychology, she was able to spot erratic driving very quickly, and by her paralysis she could offer herself as a horrible example of the consequences. During one of these forays she met a young cop named John. Her disability and disfigured face bothered him not a whit, and they had a whirlwind romance. Shortly he proposed to her. After Julie won his mother over (she had told him "he was throwing his life away by marrying a cripple"), they were married in a joyous ceremony. Rather than having a live reception, they held the reception on-line, toasting and being toasted by friends from remote sites around the country. They announced that they intended to honeymoon in the Greek islands, and soon real postcards from Greece began showing up in their friends' mailboxes.

Julie's professional life began to bloom. She began attending conferences and giving papers around the States, and shortly in Europe as well. Of course there were problems, but John was the quintessential caring husband, watching out for her, nurturing her. Her new popularity on the conference circuit allowed them to take frequent trips to exotic places. While they were on safari, if there was a place her wheelchair couldn't reach, he simply carried her. When they were home he was frequently out on stakeouts in the evenings, which gave her lots of time to engage with her on-line friends. Occasionally he would take over the keyboard and talk to her friends on the chat system.

Julie began talking about becoming a college teacher. She felt that she could overcome her handicap by using a computer in the classroom. This would be hooked to a large screen to "talk" with her students.[7] Throughout the planning of her new career, John was thoroughly supportive and caring.[8]

It was some time during this period that Julie's friends first began to become suspicious. She was always off at conferences, where presumably she met face to face with colleagues. And she and John spent a lot of time on exotic vacations, where she must also be seeing people face to face. It seemed that the only people who never got to see her were her on-line friends. With them she maintained a firm and unyielding invisibility. There were beginning to be too many contradictions. But it was the other disabled women on-line who pegged her first. They knew the real difficulties—personal and interpersonal— of being disabled. Not "differently abled," that wonderful term, but rather the brutal reality of the way most people—including some friends—related to them. In particular they knew the exquisite problems of negotiating friendships, not to mention love relationships, in close quarters with the "normally" abled. In that context, Julie's relationship with the unfailingly caring John was simply impossible. John was a Stepford husband.

Still, nobody had yet pegged Julie as other than a disabled woman. The other disabled women on-line thought that she was probably a disabled woman, but also felt that she was probably lying about her romantic life and about her frequent trips. But against that line of argument they had to deal with the reality that they had hard evidence of some of those trips—real postcards from Greece—and in fact Julie and John had gone back to Greece next year, accompanied by another flurry of postcards.

Julie, John, Joan—they are all wonderful examples of the war of desire and technology. Their complex virtual identities are real and productive interventions into our cultural belief that the unmarked social unit, besides being white and male, is a single self in a single body. Multiple personality "disorder" is another such intervention. As I tried to make clear in "Identity in Oshkosh," MPD is generally considered to be pathological, the result of trauma. But we can look to the construction and management of pathology for the circumstances that constitute and authorize the unmarked, so that we may take the pathologization of MPD and in general the management and control of any manifestations of body-self, other than the one body–one self norm, to be useful tools to take apart discourses of the political subject so we can see what makes them work. There are other interventions to be made, and here we interrogate a few Harawayan elsewheres—in this case, virtual space, the phantasmic "structure" within which real social interactions take place—for information. Of course, the virtual environment of the chat lines is just the beginning, a look at a single event when such events were still singular.

Julie's friends weren't the only ones who were nervous over the turns her life was taking and the tremendous personal growth she was experiencing. In fact, Lewin was getting nervous too. Apparently he'd never expected the impersonation to succeed so dramatically. He thought he'd make a few contacts on-line, and maybe offer helpful advice to some women. What had happened instead was that he'd found himself deeply engaged in developing a whole new part of himself that he'd never known existed. His responses had long since ceased to be a masquerade; with the help of the on-line mode and a certain amount of textual prosthetics, he was in the process of *becoming* Julie. She no longer simply carried out his wishes at the keyboard; she had her own emergent personality, her own ideas, her own directions. Not that he was losing his own identity, but he was certainly developing a parallel one, one of considerable puissance. Jekyll and Julie. As her friendships deepened and simultaneously the imposture began to unravel, Lewin began to realize the enormity of his deception.

And the simplicity of the solution.

Julie had to die.

And so events ground inexorably onward. One day Julie became seriously ill. With John's help, she was rushed to the hospital. John signed on to her account to tell her on-line friends and to explain what was happening: Julie had been struck by an exotic bug to which she had little resistance, and in her weakened state it was killing her. For a few days she hovered between life and death, while Lewin hovered, setting up her demise in a plausible fashion.

The result was horrific. Lewin, as John, was deluged with expressions of shock, sorrow, and caring. People offered medical advice, offered financial assistance, sent cards, sent flowers. Some people went into out-and-out panic. The chat lines became jammed. So many people got seriously upset, in fact, that Lewin backed down. He couldn't stand to go through with it. He couldn't stand to engineer her death. Julie recovered and came home.

The relief on the net was enormous. Joyous messages were exchanged. Julie and John were overwhelmed with caring from their friends. In fact, sometime during the great outpouring of sympathy and concern, while Julie was at death's door, one of her friends managed to find out the name of the hospital where she was supposed to be staying. He called, to see if he could help out, and was told there was no one registered by that name. Another thread unraveled.

Lewin was still stuck with the problem that he hadn't had the guts to solve. He decided to try another tack, one that might work even better from his point of view. Shortly, Julie began to introduce people to her new friend, Sanford Lewin, a New York psychiatrist. She was enormously gracious about it, if not downright pushy. To hear her tell it, Lewin was the greatest thing to hit a net since Star-Kist Tuna. She told them Lewin was absolutely wonderful, charming, graceful, intelligent, and eminently worthy of their most affectionate attention. Thus introduced, Lewin then began trying to make friends with Julie's friends himself.

He couldn't do it.

Sanford simply didn't have the personality to make friends easily on-line. Where Julie was freewheeling and jazzy, Sanford was subdued and shy. Julie was a confirmed atheist, an articulate firebrand of rationality, while Sanford was a devout conservative Jew. Julie smoked dope and occasionally got a bit drunk on-line; Sanford was, how shall we say, drug-free—in fact, he was frightened of drugs—and he restricted his drinking to a little Manischewitz on high holy days. And to complete the insult, Julie had fantastic luck with sex on-line, while when it came to erotics Sanford was a hopeless klutz who didn't know a vagina from a virginal. In short, Sanford's Sanford persona was being defeated by his Julie persona.

What do you do when your imaginary playmate makes friends better than you do?

With Herculean efforts Lewin had succeeded in striking up at least a beginning friendship with a few of Julie's friends when the Julie persona began to come seriously unraveled. First the disabled women began to wonder aloud, then Lewin took the risk of revealing himself to a few more women with whom he felt he had built a friendship. Once he started the process, word of what was happening spread rapidly through the net. But just as building Julie's original persona had taken some time, the actual dismantling of it took several months, as more clearly voiced suspicions gradually turned to factual information and the information was passed around the conferences, repeated, discussed, and picked over. Shortly the process reached a critical level where it became self-supporting. In spite of the inescapable reality of the deception, though, or rather in spite of the inescapable unreality of Julie Graham, there was a kind of temporal and emotional mass in motion that, Newton-like, tended to remain in motion. Even as it slowly disintegrated like one of the walking dead, the myth of Julie still tended to roll ponderously ahead on its own, shedding shocked clots of ex–Julie fans as it ran down. The effect, though spread out over time, was like a series of bombing raids interspersed throughout a ground war.

Perhaps to everyone's surprise, the emotion that many of those in the chat system felt most deeply was mourning. Because of the circumstances in which it occurred, Julie's unmasking as a construct, a cross-dressing man, had been worse than a death. There was no focused instant of pain and loss. There was no funeral, no socially supported way to lay the Julie persona to rest, to release one's emotions and to move on. The help Julie had given people in that very regard seemed inappropriate in the circumstance. Whatever else Julie was or wasn't, she had been a good friend and a staunch supporter to many people in need, giving unstintingly of her time and virtual energy wherever it was required. Her fine sense of humor and ability to see the bright side of difficulties had helped many people, mostly women, over very difficult places in their lives. At least some of her charm and charisma should have rubbed off on Lewin. But it didn't. And, quite understandably, some of the women did not bounce back with forgiveness. At least one said that she felt a deep emotional violation which, in her opinion, was tantamount to sexual assault. "I felt raped," she said, "I felt as if my deepest secrets were violated. The good things Julie did . . . were all done by deception." Some of the women formed a support group to talk about their sense of betrayal and violation, which they referred to wryly as "Julie-anon."

The relationship of the Julie incident to Peterson's rape of Sarah's Franny persona in Oshkosh is remarkable for its resonances. There is no mention of pathology with Lewin's Julie persona, even though the issue of rape was explicitly raised and one of Lewin's personae committed it. Conversely, in Sarah's case issues of pathology are the deciding factors, working both in her favor (Peterson was convicted because Sarah was judged mentally incompetent because of her multiple personalities) and against her (the decision implicitly places limits on Sarah's social agency). Significantly, in terms of the American system of justice, the question of pathology was never raised in connection with Peterson, who committed a physical act of rape, but was an issue in regard to his victim and was used in a kind of reverse and problematic spin to convict him. The issue of warranting was clear in Sarah's case (Malcolm Ashmore's "furniture" argument . . . the judge and jury accepted the evidence of their eyes, they could *see* Sarah relinquish the host body to the Franny persona), but its occultation in Julie's case enabled the rape (the narrow-bandwidth mode of the nets interfered with the chat participants' warranting Julie to Lewin, so that even when they became suspicious they had to fall back on nonphysical cues that failed them). The issue of presence is more tricky. The judge and jury had a single physical body to look at, but they clearly experienced the presence of several persons within that frame. The wide-bandwidth mode of physicality permitted them to warrant those personae to a specific physical individual, the politically apprehensible citizen. In Julie's case the technosocial mode of virtual systems is in full operation. Because of the limited bandwidth mode of the net, both of Lewin's personae had equal presence—but sufficient presence that participants in the chat conferences had no difficulty in distinguishing between them and in making sophisticated distinctions regarding possible friendships and mutual interests. There was no politically apprehensible citizen, but there were certainly socially legible personae.[9]

The Julie incident produced a large amount of Monday morning quarterbacking among the habitués of CompuServe's chat system. In retrospect, several women felt that Julie's helpfulness had exceeded the bounds of good sense—that what she had actually fostered was dependency. Others focused on her maneuvers for net sex, which sometimes amounted to heavy come-ons even with old friends. Perhaps most telling was the rethinking, among Julie's closest friends, of their attitudes toward Julie's disability. One said, "In retrospect, we went out of our way to believe her. We wanted to give her all the support we could, because of what she was trying to do. So everybody was bending over backward to extend praise and support and caring to this disabled person. We were all so supportive when she got married and when she was making all the speaking engagements . . . in fact there was a lot of patronizing going on that we didn't recognize at the time."

Sanford Lewin retained his CompuServe account. He has a fairly low profile on the net, not least because the Sanford persona is inherently low-key. Many of Julie's friends made at least a token attempt to become friends with him. Not too many succeeded, because, according to them, there simply wasn't that much in common between them. Several of the women who were friends of Julie have become acquaintances of Lewin, and a few have become friends. One said, "I've been trying to forget about the Julie thing. We didn't think it through properly in the first place, and many of the women took risks that they shouldn't have. But whether he's Julie or Sanford, man or woman, there's an inner person that must have been there all along. That's the person I really like."

The hackers in my study population, the people who wrote the programs by means of which the nets exist, just smiled tiredly. A few sympathized with the women whom Julie had taken in, and understood that it takes time to realize, through experience, that social rules do not necessarily map across the interface between the physical and virtual worlds. But all of them had understood from the beginning that the nets presaged radical changes in social conventions, some of which would go unnoticed. That is, until an event like a disabled woman who is revealed to be "only" a persona—not a true name at all—along with the violated confidences that resulted from the different senses in which various actors understood the term *person*, all acted together to push these changes to the foreground. Some of these engineers, in fact, wrote software for the utopian possibilities it offered. Young enough in the first days of the net to react and adjust quickly, they had long ago taken for granted that many of the pre-net assumptions about the nature of identity had quietly vanished. Even though they easily understood and assimilated conflictual situations such as virtual persona as mask for an underlying identity, few had yet thought very deeply about what underlay the underlying identity. There is an old joke about a woman at a lecture on cosmology who said that she understood quite clearly what kept the earth hanging in space; it actually rested on the back of a giant turtle. When asked what the turtle was standing on, she replied that the turtle was standing on the back of yet another turtle, and added tartly, "You can't confuse me, young man; it's turtles all the way down."

Is it personae all the way down?

Say amen, somebody.

4

Reinvention and Encounter: Pause for Theory

Having been a technical and scientific writer (or weenie) as well as an author of fantasy and science fiction, I am aware that the boundaries between science and fiction are fluid. The most troubling stories are precisely those that are difficult to analyze—stories that are situated in the boundaries between categories and that must be analyzed in multiple ways before their meanings can be understood. In the listener they frequently produce a sense of unease, a feeling that the way things are might shift unexpectedly or slip away. I find that frequently these are the most interesting stories, because their shape-shifting qualities make them powerful agents of transformation.

Different beings tell these boundary stories. Some are people (as we provisionally understand the term). Some are more or less anonymous collective agencies like governments, departments, and bureaus, where an individual's name on the story is usually a polite formality. Some stories seem to be just there, as if they materialized out of thin air. There are other beings that tell stories as well, entities that are harder to describe. However they may be constituted, we tend to see them as people like ourselves. We put faces on enormous collectivities. "The IRS screwed me." Such seemingly light remarks show our deep proclivity, our deep need, to make self in the world— usually our own self that we remake continually, but also the need to make self out of *any* collection of attributes that we think we can recognize as possessing agency . . . that is, that resembles or *acts like* our definitions of a "person."[1]

As I listen to the stories by which we produce our communities, our bodies, and our selves, my stakes are high in understanding who is telling them and for what reason. The way each of us experiences our own senses of ourselves often seems like a universal constant, unchanged across space and time. That there is an "I" within each of us is unproblematic, a given. Yet other things about ourselves that we thought of as given and immutable have proven to be quite plastic and malleable. Take, for example, the ways in which feminist theoreticians took the "fact" of sex apart into some of its components and demonstrated a multiplicity of distinctions between the concepts of sex and gender. Making gender visible was partially possible because theoreticians working in such areas as cultural and feminist studies developed new tools for changing the ways we had learned to see, to make a deeper, more fine-grained seeing possible. The just-so character of stories of gender—the very quotidian and homely character of their invisibility—helped conceal the operations of networks of power and the flow of their energies, and in a similar way the homely, given character of bodies and selves conceals networks, pervasive and powerful in their own ways. Stories of body and self and the communities they form make up much of the groundwork of our lives. I say bodies *and* selves not because we are children of Descartes, and must keep them separate—more than anything else, feminist and cultural theorists, as well as others, have begun to dislodge that grounding myth in such a way that, with luck and support from fellow travelers, it may never fall back quite into place—but because the coupling between our bodies and our selves is a powerfully contested site, densely structured, at which governments, industries, scientists, technologists, religious fanatics, religious moderates, media practitioners, and scholars fight for the right to speech, for a profoundly moral high ground, and not incidentally for the right to control the epistemic structures by which bodies mean.

Our commonsense notions of community and of the bodies from which communities are formed take as starting points, among others, that communities are made up of aggregations of individual "selves" and that each "self" is equipped with a single physical body. I tell inquiring scholars that at the Advanced Communication Technology Laboratory in the Department of Radio-TV-Film here at the University of Texas at Austin, we refer to these principles as BUGS—a body unit grounded in a self. The notion of the self as we know it, called in various studies the "I" and in others the "subject," that tenacious just-so story that goes on to assure us that there exists an "I" for each body and that while there can be more than one "I" on tap there can only be one present at any time, seems a natural and inevitable part of life. It was just this kind of story that we told each other in order to hide the complexities of gender and of what we call race, until theoreticians of gender, sexuality, and culture made the practices visible and showed how their invisibility authorized and anchored interlocking systems of oppression. There was more than enough work to be done with issues arising from gender and race to occupy an entire generation of theorists. But most Western theories of the self, even feminist theories, stop just short of tinkering with the framework upon which the idea of gender itself is based—the framework of the individual's self-awareness in relation to a physical body. It is by means of this framework that we put in place the "I" without whose coupling to a physical body there can be no race or gender, no discourse, no structure of meaning.

It is for this reason that the need to make self seems so urgent. Telling any story seems to depend upon BUGS. To make visible the stories by which the complex and shifting play of body, self, and community is continually made and remade, we need to look for the signs of the apparatus by means of which the stories are told, and, by tracing the evolution of this apparatus, we need to show the forces, battles, negotiations, and settlements by which it is made and remade.

A disabled woman types on a computer keyboard with her headstick, conversing with friends at other keyboards in the vast elsewhere of the computer conferencing nets. She offers her many women friends advice for their emotional problems, sound advice that helps them effect real and positive changes in their lives. A few years later, it is discovered that the disabled woman is a persona, a social construct created by a middle-aged, fully abled male psychiatrist. Some horrified and disgusted women repudiate the genuine gains they had made in their lives. They state that they feel the communication was insufferably dishonest. Computer hackers, mostly young white males, fail to understand what the women are upset about.

These encounters are about relationships between bodies and personae/selves/subjects, and the multiplicities of connections between them. They are about negotiating realities, and the conjunctions of social spaces and activities bound together by webs of physical and ideological force. They map out a field of discourse for which they act as experiential demarcations:

· Many persons in a single body (multiple personality).
· Many persons outside a single body (personae within cyberspace in its many forms and attendant technologies of communication).
· A single person in/outside many bodies (institutional social behavior).

The two constants in these accounts are bodies and experiences of self, whether they are called avatars, persons, selves, or subjects.

One way to read the history of technology is as a series of complexifications, knots and loosenings of the bonds and tensions between bodies and selves, mediated by technologies of communication, within a force field of power relationships—and I intend as a purposive inflection the science fiction flavor of "force fields." Over time, as technology has grown increasingly complex, and in particular with the development of information technology (which addresses itself overtly rather than covertly to symbolic exchange), the role of technology in mediating the flow of communication between bodies and selves has become more ubiquitous and more indispensable. From this situation arises a complex variety of densely structured interactions among actors and actants that resist traditional categories—such as, say, social or technical categories—and resist traditional modes of analysis. Because the character of their interactions resembles that of familiar social systems, but rather than interacting in villages, cities, or clubs they interact "virtually," in the elsewhere space of communications networks, I call them *virtual systems*.

Technologies that enable near-instantaneous communication among social groups pose old problems in new guises (similar to the unexpected ways in which the invention of the automobile affected postadolescent courting behavior in some industrialized nations), but also pose new problems: not simply problems of accountability (i.e., who did it), but of *warrantability* (i.e., did a body/subject unit do it). The issue of warrantability—that is, is there a physical human body involved in this interaction *anywhere?*—is one such.

Anselm Strauss and others[2] have argued that a group constituted around a common symbolic structure is a "culture area" of its own, "the limits of which are set neither by territory nor formal member-ship, but by the limits of effective communication."[3] In terms that work quite well for virtual systems, Strauss asserts:

We may say that every group develops its own system of significant symbols which are held in common by its members and around which group activities are organized. Insofar as the members act toward and with reference to each other, they take each other's perspectives toward their own actions and thus interpret and assess that activity in communal terms. Group membership is thus a symbolic, not a physical, matter, and the symbols which arise during the life of the group are, in turn, internalized by the members and affect their individual acts.[4]

In commenting on the work of G. H. Mead, Strauss was quick to point out the implications of such a position. The constitution and evolution of social worlds, the form and structure of community as expressed spatially in architecture and proxemics, need not be depen-dent upon distribution in a physical space the arrangement of which acquires ontic status, but instead could as validly be based upon sym-bolic exchanges of which proximity is merely a secondary effect. As complex technologies increasingly mediate communication, raising problems of accountability (e.g., obscene phone calls), theorists have turned their attention to the systems that arise within the frame of communications technologies as a source of social control and as indicators of crises and responses in the social order. Among the recent attention to following technological objects as mediators in social interaction is the work of Shirley Strum. Sharing research with Bruno Latour at UC San Diego and drawing upon her studies of baboons, Strum suggests that the first tools used by primates were other primates, and therefore the earliest technologies were social interactions, mediators in a system of symbolic exchange.[5]

Consider a study of the relationships between bodies and selves in terms of an analysis of the history of one set of practices—say, communications technologies (telegraph, telephone, radio, television, fax, ISDN, computer networks, and games) in a particular period (the twentieth century and after). Let us treat the history of these technologies as an account of dissociation and integration—of the tensions between selves and bodies and the play of their interactions, separations, and fusions. By mediating these interactions, communications technologies serve specific functions as creators and mediators of *social spaces* and *social groups*.

Social spaces and social groups do not spring into being only as concomitants of technology. Some workers study technologies as crystallizations of social networks, the technologies and the networks cocreating each other in an overlapping multiplicity of complex interactions (Cole 1989; Haraway 1990; Tomas 1989; Star 1990b; etc.). Technologies can be seen as simultaneously causes of and responses to social crisis (Wilson 1986). Consider following the history of communication technologies as a study of social groups searching for ways to enact and stabilize a sense of *presence* in increasingly diffuse and distributed networks of electronically mediated interaction, and thus also as ways to stabilize self/selves in shifting and unstable fields of power.

Let's consider bodies and selves in relation to communications technology in three ways:

1. Selves and relationships between selves constituted and mediated by technologies of communication; i.e., *an apparatus for the production of community.*

2. Technologies that mediate cultural legibility for the biological substrates to selves, substrates that legally authenticate political action; i.e., *an apparatus for the production of body.*

3. Technologies mediating between bodies and selves that may or may not be within physical proximity; i.e., *interfaces.*

Implicit in many of these accounts are assumptions about what bodies should be or do, what form bodies should take, and what conditions relationships between bodies and selves should require.

Over time, the relationship between bodies and their attendant "selves" has undergone a slow process of change. Although its effects have been profound and lasting, the classical bourgeois worldview, incorporating a mechanistic view of the universe/nature and an egoistic view of "man," with its implications for the ways body and self might be coupled under a particular set of political and epistemological constraints, was a preeminent factor in the production of knowledge for a period of only about 150 years. Its influence began to be felt perhaps in the late 1600s and was signaled by the publication of Newton's *Principia,* for example; it was challenged, though not silenced, in the 1840s at about the time of the discovery of non-Euclidean geometry and the development of critical psychology. Powerful social forces channeled the structure of this worldview into the form of binary oppositions: body/mind, self/society, male/female, and so on. In the deployment of a series of epistemes whose informing principles include the ontic status of binary oppositions, we can see both the workings of the totalizing mechanisms that produced the new classical sciences and also the substructure for the academic disciplines—the deployment of each being deeply informed by the emergence of capitalism as a primary influence upon the structures of knowledge production.

This deployment of knowledge structures was accompanied by improvements in systems of measurement both in the realms of the physical and the symbolic (as in cartography and psychology). Partly, I suggest, this process represented a complex response to a political need to order the relationships between the emerging "subject" and its presumed associated body in ways that assured the maintenance of a social order that was already in dangerous disequilibrium. In this sense of the term, social order implied spatial accountability— that is, knowing where the subject under the law was.

Accountability traditionally referred to the physical body and most visibly took the form of laws that fixed the physical body within a juridical field whose fiduciary characteristics were precisely determined—the census, the introduction of street addresses, passports, telephone numbers—the invention and deployment of documentations of citizenship in all their forms, which is to say, fine-tuning surveillance and control in the interests of producing a more "stable," manageable citizen. The subtext of this activity is an elaboration and amplification of spaciality and presence—a hypertrophy of the perception of *where,* which was reflected in the elaboration, within the sciences, of new fiduciary understandings of cosmic and molecular (and later, atomic) velocity and position.

The symmetry implied by the increasing precision with which both velocity and position could be determined in the macro and micro world was ruptured in the 1920s and '30s by the theoretical work of Niels Bohr, for example, and later by Werner Heisenberg. The deep ontic unease that these proposals generated, even though they were frequently only imperfectly understood,[6] was accompanied by increasing preoccupation on the part of a political apparatus at the macro level for precisely determining action (as speed, e.g., cf. Virilio) and position in everything from satellite ranging to postal codes. Implicit in this elaboration of the concepts of spatiality and presence is the development of the fiduciary subject, that is, a political, epistemological, and biological unit that is not only measurable and quantifiable but also understood in an essential way as being *in place.* The individual societal actor becomes fixed in respect to geographical coordinates that determine physical locus—a mode that implies an ontic privilege of the physical body and an unusual but identifiable invocation of a metaphysics of presence that may be familiar from other debates—rather than being located in a virtual system, that is, in relation to a social world constituted within an information network, a social world whose primary mode of interaction is that of narrow-bandwidth symbolic exchange. In the context of this research, by a metaphysics of presence I mean that a (living) body implies the presence within the body of a socially articulated self that is the true site of agency. It is this coupling, rather than the presence of the body alone, that privileges the body as the site of political authentication and political action.

Tactics of discipline and control directed at the body are *meant* to manage the coupled self within which agency and consequent political authenticity have been constructed to reside. The fiduciary subject is fixed and stabilized within a grid of coordinates that implicates virtual location technologies—making the boundaries between the jurisdictions of the physical and those of the symbolic extremely permeable—by techniques such as psychological testing.

In this way the deployment of the new kinds of knowledge that accompanied capital formation and of their concomitants in the arts and sciences—in particular a worldview that took for its basis a binary experiential framework—had a profound effect on perceptions of and relationships to the human body. This effect is particularly clear in regard to ways in which an individual acquired knowledge of the categories of physical experience—of experiences of one's own body. For example, the invention of sensual categories such as pleasure as ways of interpreting bodily experience in European discourses of the body—a fairly late development—can be interpreted as an attempt to impose order upon the chaotic and unruly theater of sensual experiences that the body was thought to represent, in all its disruptive and productive potential.[7] Categorizing the sensual modes that bodies can experience fulfills several functions. It elicits a discourse system; it represents efforts to frame the body as an ordered set of impressions that could be disrupted and require reordering (implying a structure to do the ordering); and it implies a binary view of the ways that bodily experience is mediated—the opposition of order and chaos within the frame of a single physicality.

On a high-resolution color computer screen appear images of a man and woman being married in an elaborate ceremony. They, their wedding party, a few presents, and the surrounding landscape appear on the screen as detailed drawings, like a cartoon movie. Some of the guests appear to be animals, while others are invisible, signaling their presence by a small cloud at the top of the screen. Each bodylike form on the screen is an avatar, a body-representative for a physical person who might be located anywhere in the world. The mainframe that makes their social interaction possible is located in Yokohama, but each person's physical body is seated at a terminal somewhere in the world; and the geography of the landscape that surrounds their wedding party is, in Haraway's terms, elsewhere.

Theorists of gender and the body view individuals' experiences of their own bodies as socially constructed, in juxtaposition to approaches which hold that the body is ontologically present to itself and to the experiences of the (always unitary) "self" that inhabits it; in Lacanian terms, under the older dispensation the essence of one's own body is understood as that which ultimately resists symbolization. If we consider the physical map of the body and our experience of inhabiting it as socially mediated, then it should not be difficult to imagine the next step in a progression toward the social—that is, to imagine the *location* of the self that inhabits the body as also socially mediated—not in the usual ways we think of subject construction in terms of position within a social field or of capacity to experience, but of the *physical* location of the subject, *independent* of the body within which theories of the body are accustomed to ground it, within a system of symbolic exchange, that is, information technology.

Theorizing a self in this way—a particular interpretation of spatiality and location, in relation to a network of information exchange through which the self moves by a different order of vectors from those by which the body moves, a self which moves in a spatiality from which the body is excluded—allows us to interpret the world of high-speed communications technology as a cultural framework within which social interaction can be understood as "normal" and can be studied in the same way as other social systems. Having made that statement, however, I must immediately move on to add that in virtual systems interactions are, after all, a bit different. So much for seamless theory. The chief difference is the effect of changing the density of the communication, or the bandwidth. Bandwidth, as I use the term here, refers to the amount of information exchanged in unit time. "Reality" is wide-bandwidth, because people who communicate face to face in real time use multiple modes simultaneously—speech, gestures, facial expression, the entire gamut of semiotics. In a wonderful exercise on emergent behavior in designing "intelligent" kitchen appliances (e.g., if appliances get to be so smart, what do they do when you're not home), Wendy Kellogg comments wryly that the current standard for bandwidth by which we judge visual communication is that of reality . . . a high bandwidth indeed. In video terms, bandwidth translates into resolution. Kellogg is fond of pointing out real objects in the lecture hall and remarking on how much resolution they have. Computer conferencing is narrow-bandwidth, because communication is restricted to lines of text on a screen.

The cultural history of electronic communication is in part a history of exponentially increasing bandwidth. The effect of narrowing bandwidth is to engage more of the participants' interpretive faculties. This increased engagement has the effect of making communication more difficult when the information needs to be conveyed precisely. On the other hand, for symbolic exchange originating at and relating to the surface of the body, narrowing the bandwidth has startling effects. A deep need is revealed to create extremely detailed images of the absent and invisible body, of human interaction, and the symbol-generating artifacts which are part of that interaction. Frequently in narrow-bandwidth communication the interpretive faculties of one participant or another are powerfully, even obsessively, engaged.

A typical example of the extent to which participants in narrow-bandwidth communication engage their own interpretive faculties and of the extent to which their interpretations are driven by the engagement of structures of desire is provided by studies of client-provider interactions in phone sex. Phone sex is the process of constructing desire through a single mode of communication, the human voice. The communication bandwidth between client and provider is further narrowed because the voices are passed through the telephone network, which not only reduces the audio bandwidth but also introduces fairly high levels of distortion. In my studies of phone sex, I was particularly interested in how distortion and bandwidth affected the construction of desire and erotics.[8]

Technically speaking, the effect of distortion on the intelligibility of the human voice has been most thoroughly studied. As one might expect, most of the studies have been conducted or commissioned by the military, as part of efforts to fix adequate standards of intelligibility for communication under battle conditions. In the process, the studies showed that the human auditory system has extremely wide tolerance for distortion and bandwidth limitation in voice communication. On the other hand, they failed to note that even small amounts of distortion create changes in interactive styles. It seems reasonable to speculate that these changes are caused by the participants' engaging their interpretive faculties in an effort to provide closure on a set of symbols that is perceived as incomplete. But closure in regard to what?

In phone sex, once the signifiers begin to "float" loose from their moorings in a particularized physical experience, the most powerful attractor becomes the client's idealized fantasy. In this circumstance narrow bandwidth becomes a powerful asset, because extremely complex fantasies can be generated from a small set of cues. In enacting such fantasies, participants draw on a repertoire of cultural codes to construct a scenario that compresses large amounts of information into a very small space. The provider verbally codes for gesture, appearance, and proclivity, and expresses these as verbal tokens, sometimes compressing the token to no more than a single word.

The client uncompresses the tokens and constructs a dense, complex interactional image. In a Lacanian interpretation of these interactions, client and provider mobilize erotic tension by taking advantage of lack—filling in missing information with idealized information. In this circumstance desire, theorized as a response to perceived lack, arises as a product of the tension between embodied reality and the emptiness of the token, in the forces that maintain the preexisting codes by which the token is constituted. The client mobilizes expectations and preexisting codes for body in the modes of experience, such as smell and taste, that are absent from the token.

Because tokens in phone sex are presented in the verbal mode alone, the client employs cues provided by the verbal token to construct a multimodal object of desire with attributes of shape, tactility, scent—in other words, all the attributes of physical presence—from the client's own experiential or phantasmic cultural schema. This act is thoroughly individual and interpretive, so that out of a highly compressed token of desire the client constitutes meaning that is dense, locally situated, and socially particular. The token has some of the attributes of a fetish, which is also a concretization of a structured interaction with an absent object that mobilizes desire or expectations of desire.

Narrow-bandwidth interactions are useful in analyzing how participants construct desire because the interactions are both real and schematized. Though they cannot provide information about the vast and complex spectrum of human sexuality across time and society, they do provide a laboratory that is large, moderately diverse, and easily accessible for a detailed study of desire in narrow-bandwidth mode. But it is not necessary to engage in interactions that mobilize desire to experience the attraction of virtual systems. In the early days of my study, an informant at an organization that tracks high-technology businesses commented that large public databases were experiencing difficulty in becoming profitable. "What's happening," he said, "is that users don't find the services, like on-line ticketing, electronic shopping, and stock reports, very interesting. On the other hand, the on-line conferences are jammed. What commercial on-line information services like Prodigy don't realize is that people are willing to pay money just to *connect*. Just for the opportunity to communicate." That Prodigy fails to understand this point is clear from the way the database runs its conferences. Prodigy supervisors monitor its on-line conferences and censor what it considers offensive language—what Latour might consider an example of building your morals into your technology and what I would consider building your morals into your nature.[9] At this point it does not look like imposing a set of morals of any kind on the net is going to work. "Centralized control is impossible," Chip Morningstar and Randall Farmer (1991) say, speaking of *Habitat,* at present the largest social experiment in virtual space. "Don't even try."

In an ironic mode, I consider that remark to be a vastly hopeful one—in part, at least, because centralized control is not the only kind of control. Just as technology, in Gibson's words, finds its uses on the street, control finds its uses in virtual systems, and I hope to observe the transformations that control undergoes as it seeks its level among the virtual communities. Virtual systems imply particular understandings of space, time, proximity, and agency. From the unease that early users of the telephone evinced when they spoke "to" another person "through" the telephone, as opposed to speaking "to" the telephone itself,[10] contrasted with the easy familiarity with which early users of the computer seized upon the opportunities for computer conferencing, we can see that people have become comfortable with the idea that there are agencies—by which I mean politically authorized personae—on the other end of a wire, and eventually that it became unnecessary to be assured that there *was* an "other end" to the wire.

Whereas, prior to electronic communication, an agent maintained proximity through texts bearing the agent's seal, and the agency the texts implied could be enforced through human delegates, in the time of electronic speech proximity is maintained through technology, and agency becomes invisible. Users of the telephone eventually took for granted that they were speaking to another person "on" the telephone.[11] It was this sense of assurance in the presence of a specific bounded unitary agency, grounded by a voice, that undergirds a gradual refiguration of the meaning of proximity. With the advent of electronically prostheticized speech, agency was grounded not by a voice but by an iconic representation of a voice, compressed in bandwidth and volume and distorted by the limitations of the early carbon-granule transducers, so as to be something more than a signature or seal on a text but far less than an embodied physical vocalization. Agency was proximate when the authorizing body could be manifested through technological prosthetics. This technological manifestation in turn implied that the relationship between agency and authorizing body had become more discursive. This process of changing the relationship between agency and authorizing body into a discursive one eventually produced the subjectivity that could fairly unproblematically inhabit the virtual spaces of the nets.

This observation brings us to the advent of the first electronic virtual communities, in which the issues of agency and proximity got their first workout.

5

Agency and Proximity:
Communities/CommuniTrees

The first virtual communities based on information technology were the on-line bulletin board services (BBS) of the mid-1970s. These were not dependent upon the widespread ownership of computers, merely of terminals; but even a used terminal cost several hundred dollars, so that access to the first BBSs was mainly limited to electronics experimenters, ham radio operators, and the early hardy computer builders.

Bulletin board services were named after their perceived function—virtual places, conceived to be like physical bulletin boards, where people could post notes for general reading. The first successful BBS programs were primitive, mainly allowing the user to search for messages alphabetically, or simply to read messages in the order in which they were posted. These programs were sold by their authors for very little, or given away as "shareware"—part of the early visionary ethic of electronic virtual communities. The idea of shareware, as enunciated by many programmers who write shareware programs, was that the computer was a passage point for circulating concepts of community. The important thing about shareware, rather than making an immediate profit for the producer, was to nourish the community in expectation that such nourishment would "come around" to the nourisher. Information, as Stuart Brand would have it, wants to be free.

Within a few months of the first BBS's appearance, a San Francisco group headed by John James and Dean Gengle, who were programmers and visionary thinkers, had developed the idea that the BBS was potentially a new kind of community, a community that James felt could transform existing society and facilitate the emergence of new social forms. The CommuniTree Group, as they called themselves, saw the BBS in McLuhanesque terms as transformative because of the ontological structure it presupposed and simultaneously created—the mode of tree-structured discourse and the community that spoke it—and because it was another order of "extension," in McLuhan's sense, a kind of prosthesis. The BBS that the CommuniTree Group envisioned was not merely a virtual locus, but an extension of the participant's instrumentality into a virtual social space.

The CommuniTree idea began in earnest when James and Gengle began discussing the possible uses to which computers might be put when they became widely and inexpensively available. These discussions took place in the early 1970s, at a time when *computer* was synonymous with *mainframe,* with large centralized units. The first of what would later be called personal computers, the Apple II and Commodore Pet, had been on the market for only a short time. These discussions, therefore, centered around mainframes—very large computers that centralized data processing operations.

James had been thinking about human-computer interaction from this perspective for some time. In 1976, human-computer interaction meant a single human interacting with a single computer. The broad range of unexplored relationships among many humans connected by a single communication channel had not yet been studied more than superficially. Work had been done at Bell Laboratories in Murray Hill, New Jersey, by a small group of researchers studying the nascent discipline of information theory as described by Claude Shannon in his pioneering work only a few years previous. They were at the stage of preliminary experimentation with message passing, using human subjects isolated in cubicles who were restricted to communicating by writing to each other on three-by-five cards. They published this work in the 1950s.

James was thinking of the situation—not quite yet in existence—of several terminals connected together simultaneously. The humans at those terminals could communicate with one another much like people on a telephone party line. In fact, there was such an arrangement at the New Jersey Institute of Technology, although it was still quite primitive and experimental. This system, called the Electronic Information Exchange System or EIES, provided some simple protocols and a command-line interface of sorts for the exchange of simple text messages among several terminals. The NJIT engineers thought of this as a clumsy alternative to the telephone, but one that might provide useful services for such things as written memos. They thought of the mainframe as a kind of common switch between the terminals. This system was traditional, and similar to telephone "frame" computers, which were nothing more than souped-up versions of the five generations of mechanical crossbar switches and the earlier step-by-step rotary switches that had constituted automated central offices since they were first introduced in the 1940s.

At this point the working metaphor was still computer as switch, and switch as tool. Mainframes, after all, were huge, centralized number crunchers to which terminals had only recently been connected. Previously, as a rule, there had been only one terminal connected to a mainframe at a time. This terminal was called the console, because it served the same function as the control console for any large and complex electromechanical device. Usually the console contained instrumentation that provided information on the state of the machine, which parts were currently working and which were not, important voltages and temperatures, and so forth. Programs and data were supplied to the console operator in the form of stacks of cards with holes punched in them. There was nothing secret about consoles; Sperry Instruments (later Sperry Rand) kept the console for its huge, vacuum-tube Univac in a show window in Manhattan while the computer was in operation. (How recent this recent past is—or perhaps how archaic computation at the University of Texas is—may be evinced by the presence of an office in the computation complex at

UT Austin that claims to still accept punch cards for computer processing jobs.)

After this period, various manufacturers were actively working on operating systems that would permit more than one program to run at once on a single mainframe, and thereby permit more than one operator to be connected at the same time. This concurrent processing scheme would lessen somewhat the time that experimenters had to wait for their jobs to run, and if they could access the mainframe directly, they could further avoid the bottleneck of the single console operator in a single location.

It seems rather fashionable these days to talk about change in terms of paradigm shifts, but something rather like that was in the air the morning that James woke up with the germ of a new and strange idea of what the mainframe was for. James sat on the edge of the bed for a few minutes sipping scalding coffee while he mulled the idea over, and then called his friend Conrad Greenstone to bounce the idea off him. What would happen, James asked, if people at remote terminals could not only post messages to each other, but could attach messages to other messages?

Greenstone thought about it for a few seconds, and then began to talk about the possibilities. They discussed the threads of the many ideas and possible conversations that might emerge from such an arrangement. Both men were aware of the early Bell Labs work on message passing, but they didn't make a conscious connection between that work and the germ of the concept they were now discussing. James suggested a practical scheme for implementing the idea, which involved keeping track of messages by means of a computational strategy known as a binary search tree. They mentioned the EIES project and talked a bit about the utility of attaching messages to each other in terms of a distributed community of discourse. Greenstone suggested that they call such a system a conference tree.

The idea was exciting, and the two men moved into action quickly. Shortly afterward, James, Greenstone, and two mutual friends, Dean Gengle and Steve Smith, committed their time and energy to form a small business that they called the CommuniTree Group. The purpose of the group was to develop James's idea into a commercial product, and simultaneously to promote the idea of electronic community that the Tree suggested.

James and Greenstone had been, in their words, "hanging around" with the Forth Interest Group, a San Francisco Bay Area association of programmers who were dedicated to writing computer code using the Forth programming language. This was a relatively recent addition to structured programming languages, unusual in its brevity and compactness as well in its use of Reverse Polish Notation, a grammar and syntax in which predicates came before subjects. The opacity which Reverse Polish sometimes brought to computer code was aptly parodied in a bumper sticker popular among Forth programmers in the Bay Area. The sticker read: "((FORTH LIKE YOU) IF) HONK THEN" (roughly, "Honk if you like Forth").

Forth was not just another computer language; to its practitioners in the Bay Area it was a crusade, a religion. It attracted more than its share of fanatics, young Top Guns of programming who felt that the language they used strongly influenced the kinds of things they could produce, and that with Forth they could do anything at all and do it better, cheaper, and faster. Forth's way of building increasingly complex statements on a base composed of a few seed phrases, a syntactical structure known as threading, made it an unusually powerful tool for very large complex structures. The downside of Forth, and one that would later cause endless grief for the young CommuniTree fanatics, was its utter opacity.

Most structured programming languages bear some sort of distant resemblance to the grammar and syntax of the English language, so that it is possible to read and perhaps dimly comprehend a program written in, say, the C programming language merely by looking at a page of it. Not so with Forth. The impossibility of this task is partly due to the primitive character of Forth's programming elements (not meant pejoratively). And it is partly due to the sheer orneriness of Forth fanatics, many of whom, almost perversely, refuse to annotate their programs to prevent them from being understood by other, possibly rival, programmers, as well as by casual readers.[1]

An example may help to make this clearer. While common practice as well as common sense dictates that procedures be given names that roughly describe their function—for example, a procedure that resets the disk drive might be called something like RESET_DISK—some Forth jockeys elect to name their procedures after obscure mythological characters or lists of cities, such as the notorious screen-redrawing procedure opaquely named LODI_NEW_JERSEY.[2] In the latter case, the programmer claimed that the illuminated pixels the procedure sometimes produced reminded him of the lights of his hometown. The ability of such practices to sabotage program debugging might be understood if one were to imagine looking at two programs, one of which consisted of procedures with names like these:

DRAW_MENU;
GET_INPUT;
ADD_TO_FILE;
PRINT_RESULT;
END

while the other said:

SLAPITUP;
BURGUNDY;
FRODO;
EARWIG;
END[3]

This quixotic character of the Bay Area Forth programmers would turn out to be a direct contributor to the sacking and destruction of CommuniTree—what might be called a kind of electronic deforestation.

Perhaps the leading advocate of Forth-as-religion was Howard Perlmutter. A young graduate of MIT who had been raised in New York, Perlmutter had migrated to California and set up a small software development company, called Softweaver, in Santa Cruz. There he surrounded himself with a cadre of brilliant, fanatical

Forth experts from the computer science program at the University of California.

In the characteristic manner of some of the early Forth communities, to Perlmutter Forth wasn't simply a programming language. Rather, it was an element within a system, a building block in an associated group of elements that, taken together, represented a complete philosophy of life. This way of life, if practiced diligently, would effect a gradual but pervasive transformation not only in the life of the practitioner, but in the greater world as well. The similarity of this idea to a broad group of spiritual practices such as Japanese martial arts is entirely appropriate. Included in the Tao of Forth as interpreted at Softweaver were rules for right diet, which for the programmers meant macrobiotics; in practice, signing on with Softweaver meant dedicating oneself to a macrobiotic diet as long as one chose to eat communally. Macrobiotics can be a fierce discipline, and backsliders and those whose purpose was less than one-pointed would occasionally escape to one of the nearby restaurants (McDonald's was a favorite) for less spiritual nourishment. Apparently the attributes of right living did not include neatness, and more often than not Softweaver's communal kitchen was cluttered with rusty pots brimming with clotted masses of days-old mung beans and sagging mounds of cooked rice deeply engaged in their own evolution into new life forms.

Softweaver was the most visibly successful of the early independent developers in the mountains. But the hills were full of programmers like Perlmutter. Hundreds of tiny vacation cabins dotted the hillsides in the San Lorenzo Valley. Many of these had been built during the 1930s and '40s, as hideaways for young successful families during the hot summers in California's Central Valley. As the 1970s rolled past, these families were approaching old age, had moved on, or had passed their mountain properties on to their children. When these properties were originally occupied, the San Lorenzo Valley had been something of a popular vacation spot. But the valley's glory had passed in the 1960s, leaving a residual population of older residents who were quite conservative in both their political and social philosophy. Many of the old, rickety, single-walled cabins were left unoccupied; and it was in these relatively inexpensive and desirably isolated structures that a significant portion of the new generation of technofreaks were beginning to settle. Thus the aging population, either retired or engaged in fairly traditional occupations, found itself cheek by jowl with a fringe community of young single people whose lives consisted of round-the-clock computer programming interspersed with occasional raucous parties. This lifestyle could be considered grounds for suspicion, and it was.

As was the custom among the programmers, who at the time were almost exclusively male, sartorial quality was not high on the list of importance. In fact, many of the computer cowboys took a perverse pride in appearing in public in their most thoroughly worn clothing. By this means they were expressing a specific social value in their community: the privilege of flouting the strict dress codes that were a requirement for people of their age who were forced to take jobs in more traditional venues. This divide was exacerbated by the exaggerated age difference between the generations in the valley. With few exceptions, the social engines of Santa Cruz County in the 1960s and '70s—the newspapers, established businesses, public gathering places, portions of government and law enforcement—were firmly in the hands of an older and markedly conservative population. This group maintained what it considered to be traditional values against what it saw as a barbarian invasion.

The programmers' situation was made worse by their superficial resemblance to the genuine hippies who had also made the mountains their home, and whose grubby, marginal, and financially precarious lifestyle was not a thin cover over graduate-level degrees and awesome technical proficiencies. The depth of this gulf was oddly invisible to most of the technofreaks. They tended to view the hippies as not only dressed like themselves but also possessed of similar talents. That the hippies had chosen to farm or make craft commodities, or for that matter to live on welfare or to steal what they needed, looked to the programmers like a provisional choice similar to their own, which could be altered or abandoned at any moment by an act of will. Many of the programmers saw their own skills as another kind of craft skill quite similar to the craft skills of the hippies, failing to understand the unconscious worldview and dense social networks that underlay the superficially simple acts of writing computer code. In brief, to the programmers the hippies were just like them.

Many of the technofreaks were part of the first wave of young programmers to hit the valley, men barely out of their teens who had cut their teeth on microprocessors like MOS Technology's 6502, which was used by both Commodore and Apple and whose instruction set was small enough that machine-level programming was attainable with relative ease. A few were expatriates from the high-energy physics community that was beginning to form around Stanford University, and within that small group an even smaller group was playing at the boundaries between field theory and religion—a boundary that for many of the early physicists, beginning in the 1900s, was quite permeable. One of these, a tiny collection of people led by ex-physicist Nick Herbert who called themselves CORE, was working on the idea—part humorous, part serious—that the entire universe was a sentient being and that the sentience of the universe was detectable—that is, that God spoke to humanity through the discipline of physics and that God's voice could be made audible through the practices of physics—not allegorically but actually, in the form of real words snatched from the void. That, as it turned out, God happened to speak English didn't worry the CORE physicists one bit.

At bottom their plan was simple. The place through which the universe's sentience could most easily leak into the ambit of human consciousness was the boundary between ordered and random phenomena. To this end, the CORE physicists constructed a series of experiments to examine events that were thought to be completely random. They chose the decay rates of certain isotopes, because the unstable atoms that make up the radioactive components of isotopes decay to more stable states at random intervals. They fed the output of their event counters through a series of filters and thence directly to a Teletype 33 printer.

The output of the printer was weirdly disturbing. Scattered amid pages of gibberish, occasional English words stood out clearly. Taken together, they didn't quite make up intelligible sentences, but they were unnervingly close. "Just needs a little more work," Herbert said.

It was in this technosocial context—Northern California during the first wave of personal computers, a milieu dense and diverse, wild and woolly, a bit crazed in places, and shot through with elements of spirituality and cultural messianism—that the members of the CommuniTree Group began their work. They claimed (correctly) that the BBS in its original form was extremely limited in its usefulness. Their reasoning was simple. The physical bulletin board for which the BBS was the metaphor had the advantage of being quickly scannable. By its nature, a physical bulletin board, composed of cork and wood, is relatively small; and even the largest are fairly manageable in terms of their size and the amount of information that can be displayed. As a result, there is not much need for bulletin boards to be organized beyond topic headings, such as "For Sale." By simply scanning them visually, a person in search of information could manage some kind of organization of the materials present on the board. But the on-line BBS, accessible by reading only one message at a time, could not be scanned in any intuitively satisfactory fashion. There were primitive search protocols in the early BBSs, but they were usually restricted to alphabetical searches or searches by key words. Later, programmers added the capability of searches by dates of posting.

The CommuniTree Group, however, proposed something radically different. What James had designed was not simply a more sophisticated search protocol, but a wholly new kind of BBS that they called a tree-structured conference, employing as a working metaphor data structures called, in computer science terms, binary tree protocols. By using the word *tree* the group managed to invoke a kind of discourse of organicity which fit easily into ongoing northern Californian discourse in the 1970s, particularly in the San Francisco Bay area and adjoining Sonoma and Santa Cruz counties. Each branch of the tree was to be a separate conference that grew naturally out of its root message by virtue of each subsequent message that was attached to it. The continuity between messages grew from whatever thread of thought each reader found interesting. Conferences that lacked participation would cease to grow, but would remain on-line as archives of failed discourse and as potential sources of inspiration for other, more flourishing conferences. Because each reader could choose a unique thread of the discourse to develop, such a reader also became ipso facto an author, and thus CommuniTree could arguably be viewed as an early on-line hypertext system.

James and his group were acutely aware that the networks and computer systems within which their utopian project was embedded were not simply controlled by, but owed their very existence to, the military/industrial/government complex to whose agendas Communi-Tree was skew. The group was not daunted by this knowledge. Rather they believed that their approach, with its emphasis on smallness and multiplicity, decentered and acephalous command structures, and relatively low-tech components, could exist within or even infect the larger, totalizing communication structures that they shared with such formidable monoliths as the Defense Advanced Research Projects Agency, or DARPA. At times they even envisioned the operation as symbiotic—an electronic crocodile bird plucking useful data from between DARPA's teeth.

With each version of the BBS system, the CommuniTree Group supplied a massive, detailed instruction manual—which was nothing less than a set of directions for constructing a new kind of virtual community. They couched the manual in radical 1970s language, giving chapters such titles as "Downscale, please, Buddha" and "If you meet the electronic avatar on the road, laserblast hir!"[4] This rich intermingling of spiritual and technological imagery took place in the context of George Lucas's *Star Wars,* a film that embodied the themes of the technological transformativists, from the all-pervading Force to what Vivian Sobchack (1987) called "the outcome of infinite human and technological progress."

It was around *Star Wars* in particular that the technological and radically spiritual virtual communities of the early BBSs coalesced. *Star Wars* represented a future in which the good guys, tiny in number and overwhelmingly outgunned, won out over vastly superior adversaries—with the help of a mystical Force that "surrounds us and penetrates us . . . it binds the galaxy together" and which the hero can access by learning to "trust your feelings"—a quintessential injunction of the early 1970s and a juxtaposition of interiority and technology that carried over into later discourses of virtual communities.[5]

CommuniTree 1 went on-line in May 1978 in the San Francisco Bay Area of northern California, one year after the introduction of the Apple II computer and its first typewritten and hand-drawn operating manual. CommuniTree 2 followed quickly. The opening sentence of the prospectus for the first conference was "We are as gods and might as well get good at it."[6] This technospiritual bumptiousness, full of the promise of the redemptive power of technology that *Star Wars'* future offered and mixed with the easy, catchall Eastern mysticism that was popular in upscale northern California, characterized the early conferences. As might be gathered from the tone of the prospectus, the first conference, entitled "Origins," was about successor religions.

The conferees saw themselves not primarily as readers of bulletin boards nor as participants in a novel discourse, but rather as agents of a new kind of social experiment. They saw the terminal or personal computer as a tool for social transformation by the ways it refigured social interaction. Conversations on a BBS were time-aliased, like a kind of public letter writing or the posting of broadsides. They were meant to be read and replied to at a time later than they were posted. But their participants saw them as conversations, nonetheless, as social acts.[7] They spoke of them as real-time interchanges that occurred in physical spaces. When asked how sitting alone at a terminal was a social act, they explained that they saw the terminal as a window into a social space. Frequently the social space was described as being "out there" (usually accompanied by an expansive wave of the hand), or sometimes "in there" (accompanied by a gesture toward the computer). When describing the act of communication, many conference participants moved their hands expressively as though typing, emphasizing the gestural quality and essential tactility of the virtual mode. They were demonstrating a perceived deep connection between the differently embodied character of virtual communication and the articulation of that communication in terms of an imagined physical locus within which an exchange of information took place between physical entities.

From these descriptions given by participants in the earliest virtual interactions, it is already clear that virtual communication required a propensity toward play or fantasy on the part of the participants, either as a precondition of the interaction or as a concomitant. Also present in the descriptions of participants was a propensity to reduce other expressive modalities to the tactile: visual and auditory information. This has remained a constant throughout my observations except in the most trivial circumstances.[8] It seemed clear that from the beginning the electronic virtual mode possessed the power to overcome its character of single-mode transmission and limited bandwidth.

While the CommuniTree conference slowly took root and began to burgeon and ramify, certain circumstances in the marketplace were conspiring to bring trouble to the nascent communities. In 1982, Apple Computer entered into the first of a series of agreements with the federal government in which the corporation was permitted to give computers away to public schools in lieu of Apple's paying a portion of its federal taxes.

In terms of market strategy, this action dramatically increased Apple's presence in the school system and set the stage for Apple's domination of the education market. This success says more, perhaps, about IBM's clumsy approach to its own personal computer market than it does about Apple's marketing skill. In terms of raw percentage, Apple never controlled more than perhaps 30 percent of the educational market, but the remaining 70 or so percent was composed of hundreds of small domestic and foreign companies that manufactured IBM-compatible machines, or "clones." In terms of volume sales, Apple's share of the personal computer market represented only a small fraction of IBM's own machines, meaning PCs manufactured by IBM itself rather than PC-compatible machines manufactured by independent third-party companies. But Apple consistently perceived the market differently from IBM. Where IBM doggedly concentrated on business management and mainframes, Apple went after business employees, the educational market, and small, distributed systems. It was not until late in 1992 that Apple's sales volume overtook and passed IBM's, at which point Big Blue could do little more than gape in astonishment. The stranglehold that IBM had held on the computing machine business since the 1920s, beginning with the earliest Hollerith card readers for the Census Bureau, ended in 1992 because IBM's management had failed to perceive and, once perceived, to believe in the transition to distributed processing that had been under way for more than ten years. It is hardly necessary to add that the peculiar invisibility that distributed processing had for IBM extended to its concomitants as well . . . in particular to the prosthetic social implications of networked local machines.

Within a fairly brief time following Apple's successful deal with the IRS there were significant numbers of personal computers accessible to students of grammar school and high school age. Some of those computers had modems.

The students, at first mostly boys with the linguistic proclivities of pubescent males, soon discovered the Tree's phone number and wasted no time in logging onto the conferences. They appeared uninspired by the relatively intellectual and spiritual air of the ongoing debates, and they proceeded to express their dissatisfaction in ways appropriate to their age, sex, and language abilities.

The first time this adolescent discontent was expressed came as a complete surprise to the sysop. Quite suddenly, there in the middle of one of the ongoing discussions of the nature of human society and religion was a brief message:

JAMIE YOU SHITHEAD HAHAHAHAHAHAHA

As this message scrolled by, the computer beeped. Puzzled and a bit annoyed, the sysop punched keys to read the message again. Again the computer beeped. The message's author had put a control character at the end, an invisible character that caused *the computer itself* to do something—in other words, that bypassed the sysop's authority to control the machine's hardware and instead operated it directly.

The sysop scrolled to the next message:

FUCK YOU MOTHERFUCKER SHITFUCK

This time there was a whole slew of beeps after the message—20 or 30 of them—and the sysop's baby, asleep in her crib near the window, woke up at the unexpected sound and began to cry.

More annoyed now, the sysop quickly deleted both messages and went off to soothe her child. But in CommuniTree not even the sysop could actually delete a message; instead, she did a thing called exiling, by which a message is rendered invisible but remains attached to its branch. An exiled message can still be read by people who know it is there. This ability is a powerful device for preventing censorship, because any member of the Tree community who knew that messages had been exiled could simply post, or ask others to post, the exiled messages' numbers or titles.

What the sysop had temporarily forgotten was that even though exiled messages cease to be visible, they still take up disk space. When the Tree gods designed the mass storage part of the system, Apple had just released the first floppy drives and DOS software for the Apple II. The drives were fairly reasonable in cost, in part because Shugart's development of the control card was behind schedule, forcing Steve Wozniak and Randy Trigg to implement some functions in the software that would otherwise have been incorporated into the drives themselves. Each drive was capable of storing 150 kilobytes of data. CommuniTree 1 had the luxury of having two of them, and at the time 300 kilobytes of real estate looked like it extended to the farthest reaches of the universe. The Tree gods were exultant. "Three hundred K?" they said. "We'll never fill those suckers up!"

Heh heh.

One morning not long afterward the sysop was awakened by the alarming clackety-clack and baritone buzz of the Apple's drives repeatedly seeking track zero—a sound about as soothing as running a screwdriver down a wooden venetian blind. It is a dreaded noise which usually means that a disk has become defective or information has been lost. It also woke the baby again, which didn't improve the sysop's mood.

Sure enough, the Tree was down, with a "Disk Full" message. Puzzled, the Sysop punched up the data, and the Tree system reported that the number of messages on the Tree was about the same as it had been a few days previous. This made no sense, until the Sysop recalled that the Tree's operating system didn't include exiled messages in its summary of disk usage—but the Apple's DOS did. Then she remembered that there had been an unusually high number of annoying garbage messages over the past week or two. She had quickly exiled them without paying much attention, but it seemed in retrospect that there had been quite a few.

Quitting the Tree program, she booted DOS and checked the disks. A quick calculation showed that about 160 K was being used for conferencing, but another 150 K or so was being eaten up by exiled messages. She thought back about how many words long one of the little suckers usually was, and calculated that there must have been . . . ummm . . . *500* of them!

Was that possible? Yes, it was. The exiled messages had actually been arriving at the rate of about 25 a day. Because they were mindless, she'd dealt with them in a mindless fashion, frequently able to exile them in bunches because they arrived that way. Quietly and unobtrusively, this invisible garbage heap had grown until it took up all of the available space on the disks.

Now for the first time in the history of the Tree there was a need not merely to exile messages but to actually, physically, *remove* them. There was a disk maintenance routine for physically removing exiled messages, but the Tree gods had deliberately made it difficult to execute in order to discourage censorship. It involved deleting the sectors on the disk that contained the messages, then packing the remaining messages closer together. This procedure, called defragmenting, was somewhat dangerous. It involved moving the entire contents of the disk, one sector at a time, from one location on the disk to another. Of course, it introduced the possibility of catastrophic errors in the process. A single power-line spike or a tiny defect in the surface of the disk could cause the result of the defragmenting process to be nothing but garbage. Consequently, the disks had to be backed up before they were defragmented in case all the data were lost. All these factors lumped together meant that in practice it took something like two hours of the sysop's time to remove exiled messages. Originally James and Gengle figured that the process would need to be carried out perhaps once a month. With the arrival of the kiddie system killers, that rate zoomed to something like once a week, and then continued to escalate until it reached a rate of nearly once a *day*.

The sysop called in the Marines: James and Gengle. No, they said, they couldn't change the code. The Tree was the Tree—visionary, but vulnerable. And Forth was Forth—compact, but opaque.

The ideal sysop would simply have kept at it. But in practice the Tree sysop had a life, and a baby, and a job; and two hours of time a day just for removing messages—compounded as it frequently was by defragmentation failures, worn-out disks, and the consequent need to start over—rapidly grew out of control. Within a short time the Tree was jammed with obscene and scatalogical messages. Because of the provisions for privacy built into the code there was no way to monitor the messages as they arrived, and because of the anti-censorship precautions there was no easy way to remove them once they were in the system. The entire set of disks had to be purged—using up hours of time—every day or two.

Members of the Tree discourse began to fall away.

Things got worse. The young hackers discovered the sport of crashing the system by discovering bugs in the system command structure. The Tree gods had unwittingly made this task easy for them. First, because control characters passed through CommuniTree's system transparently and on into the command interface of the Apple itself, hackers could directly control the Apple's hardware from their remote machines. Second, because of the provisions of the system that made observing incoming messages impossible, the hackers were free to experiment with impunity, and there was no way for the system operator to know what was taking place until the Tree crashed.

Not all the young experimenters necessarily wanted to wreck the conferences, but entering control codes into the Apple's operating system from a remote location was an exploratory operation similar to swinging a crowbar in a darkened pottery factory—the outcome was chancy, but the odds were that it would turn out to be destructive. More to the point, it seemed clear that there was a huge frisson in the hackerkids' newfound power to destroy things at a distance, anonymously and at no risk to themselves; and this point should not be lost on those who study the conduct of war in the age of intelligent machines.

Each time the CommuniTree system melted down under the hackerkids' relentless assaults, it was generally too late to save the existing disks. The sysop would be obliged to reconstitute the ongoing conferences from earlier backup versions. This wearisome task was immensely frustrating to the conferees, who lost their paths through the discussions each time a recovery from older disks was necessary.

After only a few months of nearly continual assault that the system operators were powerless to prevent, the Tree expired, choked to death by a kind of teenage mutant kudzu vine, a circumstance that one participant saw as "the consequences of unbridled freedom of expression." CommuniTree 1 died on the floor of a house in Soquel,

California, on a sunny afternoon, its electronic guts hanging limply out onto the rug, its exhausted floppy drives still clacking, searching for tracks that were no longer readable.

However, with the Tree's final death, several young participants took the lessons and implications of such a community away with them—including the hard lessons about what was and what was not possible in an unstructured and unprotected conferencing environment, painfully learned through direct experience with the system bashers—and proceeded to write their own conference systems. Within a few years there was a proliferation of on-line virtual communities with perhaps less visionary character but with vastly superior message-handling capability—for example, Pyrzqxgl, XBBS, Temple of Zuul, PC-Tree, and the Sea of Mists—systems that had large hard drives (at the time "large" meant 40 megabytes, which is minuscule by our fin de siècle standards but still almost 200 times more storage than CommuniTree 1 possessed); that incorporated provisions for simultaneous multiple logons (e.g., Stuart II, although chat was not yet possible); that allowed monitoring and disconnection of "troublesome" participants (hackers attempting to crash the system); that were written in accessible code; and that facilitated easy removal of messages that did not further the purposes of the system operators.

Accompanying the arrival of the second generation of on-line conference software for the virtual communities was the age of surveillance and social control. This is not to say that surveillance and control did not already exist in the nets. The earliest on-line network, ARPANET, was funded and sponsored by the Department of Defense. It is widely believed that the National Security Agency, an agency of the U.S. government, routinely monitors all of the networks. In contrast, what the later conferences put in place was local surveillance instituted and monitored by individual system operators in the interests of facilitating communication for the greatest number of users. Who is sponsoring surveillance of what and for which ends, how the needs of public and private users interact, and how these agendas overlap and conflict, will become clearer as this study progresses.

In retrospect, the visionary character of CommuniTree's philosophy proved an obstacle to the Tree's survival. Ensuring privacy in all aspects of the Tree's structure and enabling unlimited access to all conferences within the Tree did not work in a context of increasing availability of terminals to young men who did not necessarily share the Tree gods' ideas of what counted as community. As one Tree veteran put it, "The barbarian hordes mowed us down." Thus, in practice, surveillance and control proved necessary adjuncts to maintaining order in the early virtual communities. The institution of virtual frontier justice in the second generation of conferences was carried out in clear knowledge of the fate of CommuniTree 1, and with considerable attention to the implications of a benevolent-despot approach to system administration. It is tempting to speculate about what might have happened if the introduction of Communi-Tree had not coincided with the first wave of computerjugend. Would quiet anarchy have prevailed for a longer time, or, given the possibility of a more gradual evolution toward more structured social order, would it perhaps have prevailed forever? Perhaps the future of electronic virtual communities would have been quite different.

Not all environments in the next generation of communities were based on conversation. An entire category of virtual environments was based on action. These were the adventure games, the multiple-user dungeons. Many of these were structured as games, but a few were begun simply as environments to explore. The pioneers of this genre, Pavel Curtis at PARC and Amy Bruckman at MIT, were both researchers who were interested in what would happen when people were turned loose in unstructured virtual environments that mimicked familiar environments in the physical world. To this end each chose mundane models; Curtis's LambdaMOO was modeled on his own home, and MediaMOO is a model of the actual MIT Media Lab.[9]

At least one environment has gone considerably beyond the text-based idea of interaction to a fully graphic interface: Fujitsu *Habitat*, in Tokyo, designed by Chip Morningstar and Randall Farmer. *Habitat* residents, who are called avatars, can change clothes and body parts. Within the simulation, the terms used to describe the framework for these changes are worth remarking: An avatar goes to the "spray shop" to buy body colors or clothes (the Japanese description is ambiguous as to which), to the "head shop" to buy a new head, but to the "sex change clinic" to change sex. Changing heads is a commercial transaction, but changing sex is a medical one, a different register of social order, even when what is being changed is a representation created with binary code.

Fujitsu employs a number of people as system administrators. The official Fujitsu descriptor for system administrators is Oracles; in attempting to explain what they do, Oracles use such terms as "dieties" and "gods of *Habitat*." Morningstar and Farmer's term was Wizards—demonstrating the emergent virtual social environments' origins in and debt to the earlier Dungeons and Dragons role-playing games. Oracles practice management by wandering around, so they are frequently active within the simulation.

Oracles are able to observe both the official records of who has signed up for *Habitat* and also who is inside the simulation. Based upon Fujitsu's figures and also upon the Oracles' and my own observations, the ratio of men to women from the "real world" who sign up for space in *Habitat* is four to one. However, among the avatars who participate in the simulation, the ratio of men to women is three to one. *Habitat* Oracles like to interpret these data as indicating that "the people who are using Fujitsu *Habitat* are selecting their *Habitat* gender without much relation to their actual gender." This is a slight misunderstanding of the data; if participants in *Habitat* selected their genders without much relation to their actual genders, the ratio of men to women would run closer to one to one. Some of the avatars are selecting genders that may be at variance with their usual gender presentations, but more likely what the figures show is that there are more men who prefer to use feminine gender presentations than there are women who prefer to use the masculine. The reasons seem the same as those in the text-based virtual communities: On-line, women attract more interest and get more attention, whether because of or in spite of their smaller numbers. "Real-world" men quickly notice this fact and appropriate it for their own advantage. Because they understand the role-playing aspects of gender presentation in the ludic space of the simulation, and because their sense of personal gender is warranted or anchored in their own bodies, and also importantly because the bandwidth limitations of the *Habitat* simulation preclude detailed, complex gender presentations, they are able to avail themselves of the advantages of gender switching without incurring the disadvantages. They enjoy the attractive and pleasurable qualities of being othered without having to experience the oppression and disempowerment that are part of its construction as well. Should any unpleasant or even incipiently boring events arise, they can simply log out. It is perhaps this ability more than anything else—the ability to log out—that feminist analysts of virtual systems find most rankling, and certainly with sufficient reason. Would that we could all log out of our oppressions or our unpleasant social situations.

In *Habitat,* avatars frequently know that their avatar friends have multiple personae, but they still manage to treat each persona as if it were a discrete individual. One Oracle said, "Other characters, even while recognizing that A-san equals B-san, will go ahead and treat him [*sic*] like a different person. I suppose that it is in these areas that in systems like Habitat we can identify role playing."

Habitat's economic dimension makes monetary exchanges possible, and in any money economy it is likely that sex will be one of the items for sale. Sex workers exist in *Habitat,* in an environment where sex, insofar as we can call it sex, is free of disease. The most common kind of (quasi)physical erotic stimulation is fellatio. So far this is invariably transacted between a male client and a woman provider. The client avatar sits in a chair, and the sex-worker avatar kneels in front of him to perform fellatio with rapid movements of her head. *Habitat* does not (yet, perhaps) evince any male sex workers, in contrast to such steamy virtual environments as the *Minitel Pink* service. It is not impossible that alternative sex practices outside the mainstream Japanese heterosexual norm could emerge, but given the character and social training of the major number of people who have access to *Habitat,* such a development is not likely to occur very soon. Tokyo's lone lesbian bar is still an isolated site of resistance in a sea of what appears to be (perhaps deceptively) stolid sexual conformity.[10]

Lessons of the Virtual Communities

The participants of these electronically mediated virtual communities acquire skills that are useful for the virtual social environments developing in late-twentieth-century technologized nations. The participants learn to delegate their agencies to body representatives that exist in imaginal spaces contiguously with representatives of other individuals. They become accustomed to what might be called lucid dreaming in an awake state—to a constellation of activities much like reading, but an active and interactive reading, a participatory social practice in which the actions of the reader have consequences in the world of the dream or of the book. The older metaphor of reading undergoes a transformation in a textual space that is consensual, interactive, and haptic, and that is constituted through inscription practices—the production of microprocessor code. The boundaries between the social and the "natural" and between biology and technology take on the generous permeability that characterizes communal space in the most recent virtual systems.

6

The End of Innocence, Part I:
Cyberdämmerung at the Atari Lab

Many virtual reality (VR) engineers believe that the first workers to build successful systems incorporating principles that could be considered cyberspace-like were Scott Fisher, Ivan Sutherland at MIT, and Tom Furness for the Air Force.[1] In 1967 and 1968, Sutherland built a see-through helmet at the MIT Draper Lab in Cambridge, Massachusetts. This system used television screens and half-silvered mirrors, so that the environment was visible through the TV displays. It was not designed to provide a surround environment. In 1969 and 1970, Sutherland continued this work at the University of Utah, doing things with vector-generated computer graphics and maps, still see-through technology. In his lab were Jim Clark, who went on to start Silicon Graphics, and Don Vickers.

Tom Furness had been working on VR systems for 15 years or more—he started in the mid-1970s at Wright-Patterson Air Force Base. His systems were also see-through, rather than enclosing. He pushed the technology forward, particularly by adopting the use of high-resolution CRTs. Furness's system, designed for the USAF, was an elaborate flight simulation cyberspace employing a helmet with two large CRT devices, so large and cumbersome that it was dubbed the Darth Vader helmet. He left Wright-Patterson in 1988 to start the Human Interface Technology Lab at the University of Washington.

Scott Fisher started at MIT in the machine architecture group. The MA group worked on developing stereo displays and crude helmets to contain them, and it received a small proportion of its funding from DARPA. When the group terminated the project, they gave the stereo displays to another group at the University of North Carolina, which was developing a display device called the Pixel Planes Machine. In the UNC lab were Henry Fuchs and Fred Brooks, who had been working on force feedback with systems previously developed at Argonne and Oak Ridge national labs. The UNC group worked on large projected stereo displays, but was aware of Sutherland's and Furness's work with helmets and experimented with putting a miniature display system into a helmet of their own. Their specialties were medical modeling, molecular modeling, and architectural walk-through. The new computer science building at UNC was designed partially with their system. Using their software and three-dimensional computer imaging equipment, the architects could "walk through" the full-sized virtual building and examine its structure. The actual walk-through was accomplished with a treadmill and bicycle handlebars. The experiment was so successful that during the walk-through one of the architects discovered a misplaced wall that would have been very expensive to fix once the actual structure had been built.

Attracted, as were many other innovators, by the charismatic leadership of Alan Kay, Fisher went to work for the Atari Corporation in 1982. Fisher's colleague Brenda Laurel, already ensconced at Atari but not yet in the lab, had been blitzing him with information about the horizons just opening there. Truth to tell, the prospects were mouthwatering; Atari, at the time an enormously wealthy company, was offering a genuine opportunity for serious work at the cutting edge of interaction research. For Fisher and for many other young, brilliant researchers, the challenge was irresistible—and, as it would turn out, dangerous.

The Atari Research Lab was a unique, controversial, and explosively short-lived organization for basic research in virtual reality and interactive multimedia in the early 1980s. It was a child of the Atari Corporation, one of the first manufacturers of personal computers and interactive game software. The lab was founded in the context of Atari's runaway growth and astonishing profitability. It was the time of the me generation—the florescence of the yuppies, the "I Want My BMW" kids, junk bonds, wholesale corporate looting, the gutting of the social services infrastructure in the United States, and the reelection of Ronald Reagan. The Republicans were in control, and the dancing looked like it would go on forever. It was a time of high corporate optimism, and within this framework two revolutionary research establishments were started up almost simultaneously. One was the modestly named World Center for Computer Research, in Paris. The World Center was the brainchild of Jean-Jacques Servan-Schreiber, who had persuaded President Georges Pompidou of the program's importance. Pompidou had then pushed the funding for the center through otherwise impenetrable red tape with gratifying speed. The other research center was the Atari Lab, on the other side of the globe but in concept and execution a universe away.

Servan-Schreiber had two candidates in mind for the prestigious directorate of the World Center. One was Seymour Papert, who had done so much groundbreaking research in computer cognition with Marvin Minsky. The other was Nicholas Negroponte, the suave and charismatic founder of the Architecture Machine Group at MIT and, later, of the Media Lab.

When Atari decided in late 1981 to start a laboratory to do research in interactivity, the impression they gave was that the Lab would be an effort on a par with nothing less than the World Center. Its scientists would have a free hand and unlimited resources to work at the cutting edge of new technology. Top management at Atari allocated spacious digs in the company's Sunnyvale, California, complex, a group of gleaming new buildings built around a sunny atrium complete with burgeoning tropical plants and singing birds. Now they needed someone to spearhead the new effort. They knew Negroponte's track record and dispatched an emissary to offer him the position of chief scientist at the new lab, only to find that he had just accepted Servan-Schreiber's offer of the directorate at the World Center. Atari immediately went to the second person they'd had in mind: Alan Kay, formerly of Xerox.

Kay had been a child prodigy and later a professional musician before being hired by Xerox when PARC was still a dream research site, lavishly funded by Xerox's huge profits. He had made an indelible mark in the industry by describing (the state of the art did not permit him to build) a handheld graphical interface computer. As they did with a whole succession of brilliant and eminently marketable ideas, Xerox missed developing the device into a marketable product.[2] Kay had also designed one of the earliest object-oriented programming languages and in other ways had distinguished himself as an up-and-coming researcher with organizational abilities.

Kay began by hiring a slew of recent MIT graduates and near graduates. Then he proceeded to raid the MIT Architecture Machine Group, luring the bright, eager young graduate students with (quite real) promises of gorgeous offices, state of the art equipment, California climate (which looked paradisiacal to the Boston-based students), and what looked like unlimited funding. They accepted in droves. "Rumor at MIT was that Alan was bringing them out in busloads," Jim Dunion said. "He took almost everybody they had. It was like draining a swimming pool."

Already at Atari was a young and brilliant researcher named Brenda Laurel. Laurel came to Atari with an M.F.A. in acting/directing. Previously she had been designing and programming interactive animated fairy tales at CyberVision, which had been giving her ideas about a doctoral dissertation.[3] She had been hired to design educational software for the brand-new home computer, and when the computer division began growing explosively, she soon found herself managing software marketing for the home computer division. She was also laying low, pretending not to know much about programming because she'd discovered it was a dangerous skill for a woman in the marketing division to possess. She'd already gotten into trouble with Ray Kassar, a VP there. When they met one afternoon he'd asked about her background, and she'd said she knew some code.

He had glowered, pointed his finger at her, and said, "You're a *programmer*." Clearly implied in his voice was "One of *those*."

This remark should have tipped Laurel off, but things were new and confusing and there were a lot of them for a young recruit to absorb. Kassar was referring to the hackers in the software division, young men in their late teens and early twenties, the first generation of their kind, who lived their lives perpetually in semidarkened rooms, sleeping at their terminals or under tables, and seemingly subsisting entirely on nothing more than Fritos, Coca-Cola, and wild determination. These crazies wore ancient Adidas and malodorous T-shirts with the sleeves ripped out, spoke a jazzy argot which was unintelligible to the suits, and—most offensive of all—pulled down salaries in the $50,000 to $60,000 range for what looked like nothing more than *playing games*. But in spite of all this they were untouchable, because it was entirely upon these disreputable and largely indecipherable quantities that the phenomenal success of Atari was based. Management felt that to tamper with the game designers' work habits might turn out to be something like defusing a bomb.

Atari had been started by the entrepreneur Nolan Bushnell in the mid-1970s. Bushnell meant to develop what at the time was being called a home computer, which, it was thought, was something that people would use to balance checkbooks and keep track of recipes—an extremely popular idea at the time, and the very things that personal computers did *not* wind up doing. Atari's machines achieved great popularity not because they could balance checkbooks but because they ran game software, very simple things involving chasing moving cursors and knocking bricks out of walls. The game software grew in sophistication with tremendous speed, and when the company was showing a nice profit Bushnell sold out. His purchaser of choice was the newly formed Warner Communications. A large interest in Warner had been quietly acquired in the early 1960s by the Kinney Group, originally a chain of parking lot franchises and shoe stores and, it was said, a respectable conduit for Mafia money during the "legitimizing" of Mafia interests that Mario Puzo described in fictional terms in *The Godfather*. With that backing, Warner was out to control as much of the entertainment business as it could.[4] Atari seemed a good choice. Bushnell had built it soundly with selling it in mind, and it was solidly profitable. Shortly, though, Warner found that it was hanging onto the tail of a financial rocket.

Atari's success was phenomenal, even to Atari. The statistics were stunning—Atari had *doubled in size every eight months three times in a row*, the largest growth ever posted by an American corporation. Nobody in management quite believed it, and nobody could explain it. Three years after acquiring Atari from Nolan Bushnell, Warner Communications was making more money from computer games than they were making from their entire extensive library of films. To some of the old hands on the financial side of the company, growth on that scale was frightening. "They thought Atari was some kind of creature like the blob in Woody Allen's *Sleeper*," Dunion said. "They thought they had climbed onto something that was totally out of control." The investment in equipment and packaging necessary to produce a new game was infinitesimal, so profits were enormous and still growing exponentially.

Which was why, when Dunion asked Alan Kay how much money Atari was going to commit to long-range research during the next ten years, Kay replied seriously, "An *infinite* amount."[5]

In fact, the company initially budgeted $15 million for the lab, which probably did look like a nearly infinite amount to the first wave of young researchers.

Atari's initial profitability had been based on the revenues from a single arcade game, in fact on one of the prototypical arcade games of all time: *Pac-Man,* which within an extremely short time found its way into not just every arcade, but also every bar, pool hall, lounge, and convenience store in the world. Nobody at Atari had any idea why *Pac-Man* was so extraordinarily successful. "Why people were willing to pay so much money for it is still a mystery," Brennan said. Michael Naimark added, wistfully, "Maybe it really *was* the magic of interaction."

Pac-Man was also the bellwether of Atari's true marketing philosophy. Bushnell had discovered the enormous potential of the game market by accident, but Atari's staggering success at it gave the company the sheen of an innovative, cutting-edge organization, ready to take risks in a new and untried field. The reality was quite different. Atari was staffed from top to bottom with suits—extremely conservative people. Essentially they were solid businessmen like Ray Kassar, people with proven management skills but little imagination. Almost to a man they were deeply skeptical, and in some cases actively afraid of the programmers. They expressed the belief that the present situation—that is, the programmers' unwholesome lifestyle and working habits—was merely a brief interlude, such as any startup might experience. Shortly, they believed, they would introduce correct operating procedures, as per, say, Lever Brothers' manual of procedures. They intended to carry this intention out by assuring that the people at supervisory level were folks with the right ideas about how good software should be written. They held meetings in which they thought about who *really* understood software management. Therefore, given their own training, it was inevitable that they recruited project managers from places with good, solid histories of developing *real* software—companies with proven track records and dependable profitability—companies like Lockheed, General Dynamics, Martin Marietta, and McDonnell Douglas.

Soon Atari had project managers who drank coffee out of personalized Cruise Missile mugs directing interactive entertainment software projects. The skills they brought to the game market were acquired by designing missile launchers and tank guidance controls. They saw no particular difference between missile software and interactive games. After all, they said, both were software. In this attitude the management hierarchy at Atari demonstrated in another way their misunderstanding of the stakes, of the links between programming styles and product, and—perhaps most urgently—of the critical differences in manufacturing style between military software and entertainment software. The timelines and reliability requirements for military software are frequently created in a pork-barrel milieu. The software has to be extremely reliable, although in practice no software is completely reliable. The projects are frequently immense, and therefore the project managers break the software up into chunks and parcel the writing out to teams. While it is possible to have a general overview of the project, the individual teams don't know precisely what the other teams are doing on the level of the code itself. And, as with any large project, any changes anywhere in the system must have a paper trail—revision requests, authorizations, confirmations. These are well-worn and quite serviceable histories of successful large-project management.

Because these things take time and are frequently designed to be expensive, project managers who have spent the greater part of their lives doing them have their own eclectic ideas of what constitutes a successful software project. The three most pertinent here are that in the era of slide rules, producing ten lines of Fortran (now Ada) code a day was about the right speed; that a workday was eight hours long; and that the average project was expected to take about four years to complete. The four-year estimate did not include after-delivery debugging and continued revision, which might be billed separately, and there was a tacit and not unreasonable assumption that after-delivery revisions will be not optional but necessary.

These Lockheed stalwarts of the military suddenly found themselves managing projects that not only had to work right the *first* time, but also had to be *fun* and had to be completed in about *six months*. For the coders, they of the flying fingers and shredder lifestyle, a typical workday might have been 20 hours. Traditionally, most of those hours were at night. Perhaps only a few hours coincided with the project manager's workday. This fact alone made traditional supervisory techniques, rooted in a nineteenth-century prospectus of continuous visual surveillance, maddeningly impractical. The coders wrote in assembly language and, in the case of the occasional rabid aficionado, in machine language. They employed every arcane trick imaginable to circumvent the obscure problems that plagued all the first- and second-generation microprocessors and thereby to make their code run faster and snazzier—tricks like self-modifying code, and code that took advantage of undocumented traps and weirdnesses in the chips' subcode[6]—which the manufacturers of the chips sternly forbade, because the weirdnesses that made such short-cuts possible might have disappeared without warning in the next manufacturing run.[7] But because the games were written to be out there in the market *now*, the chips that the programmers used were the same as the ones in the machines that the end users had; they expected to play the games for a while and then throw them away in favor of the next ones.

This tight coupling between writing a game quickly and playing it only until its potential was exhausted included such factors as practical code size (which was dictated by the capacity of the chips in the game cartridge and the computer's RAM), the programmer's stamina, and also management's and programmers' sense of what the games were for and what markets they served. Because of the tightness of the coupling, it was possible to produce games whose performance could exceed what the hardware manufacturers thought were the capacities of their equipment. For the same reason, close managerial supervision over the actual coding was both irrelevant and unhelpful. In the circumstances, Atari's mistake was quite natural: Management was thinking *product;* the coders and gamers were thinking *fun.* For an incredible few years, through an unlikely congeries of circumstances, those two conflicting attempts to control the meaning of the term *interactive entertainment software* were juxtaposed. As events would prove, for Atari the coincidence was just that: accident. While Time Warner itself was acutely aware that fun can be packaged, Atari managment simply didn't get it.

People in places like the MIT Media Lab knew about this conflict because they had been intensely interested in how Bushnell got the vision to start a company that marketed interactive software on such a grand scale. Consequently, they were aware of the reality—that Atari was not a visionary company, merely a stunningly lucky one.

With the sole exception of *Pac-Man,* Atari might as well have been in the furniture business.

Thus it was that the best and brightest perceived Atari's hiring of Alan Kay to start a research lab as a major breakthrough in Atari's humdrum conservatism, a sign that there were people at Atari who had the vision to use the enormous profits *Pac-Man* was generating to fund more and better experiments with interaction. In truth, they had misunderstood what was happening. Atari had hired Alan Kay because the company had grossly misperceived his abilities. They saw him not as a brilliant innovator but rather as a good administrator of exotic talent, someone who could keep bright programmers in line and producing. *Pac-Man,* as it quickly developed, was Atari's Maginot Line, the standoff point between the suits and the researchers. The Atari board of directors' idea of a "visionary future" was an endless series of *Pac-Man* clones, like the movie sequels that Sly Stallone had turned into a mini-industry: *Pac-Man II, Pac-Man III, Bride of Pac-Man, Pac-Man Meets Godzilla,* and so on. The company's administration thought they were buying a group of programmers who would quickly produce an endless series of *Pac-Man* spinoffs.

Collisions were not long in arriving. Ray Kassar announced his intention to spend 90 percent of the home computer software budget on licenses for games. These would run on the Atari home computer, not on the Atari game machine—which Laurel felt was a serious problem, because as yet there was nothing but game software for the home computer, and at the rate Kassar was burning through the budget there wouldn't be any other software for the home computer that year. The problem, Laurel felt, was product differentiation. Was there a difference between the home computer and the game machine? What were the differences? What was a home computer supposed to be, anyway, and why would anybody buy one if all it did was run the same software that a game machine did but cost twice as much? To get a satisfactory level of product differentiation, for openers Atari needed to have software like an 80-column word processor and a decent spreadsheet for the machine.

Kassar brushed arguments like this aside. Good licenses, he said, were what made a successful machine. He meant licensing of prominent names—the same sort of thing any mass-market company would do—and putting them on the product, like Batman towels and Batman coffee mugs. From a marketing standpoint, he said, there was no difference between Batman towels and Batman games. People bought the name, not the contents. Significantly, Kassar never talked about what the games would *do*. In this, as it developed, his reasoning was right in line with that of the rest of Atari's management.

The trouble lay in the innocuous word *research,* which each side understood quite differently. To the potential lab staff, many of whom were still at MIT doing graduate work when they were hired, research meant innovation, taking risks, doing new things. To Kassar and to the rest of Atari, research meant duplication, slight changes on an already accepted idea, but finding out how to duplicate their successes better and cheaper. Kay did not perceive this difference at first, and after he had figured it out he arranged to be away from the lab on business most of the time. By the time he did figure it out, though, the Atari administration and the lab kids were at each others' throats. "Research" was probably a boundary object in Susan Leigh Star's sense, but it didn't help the groups translate their work for each other; instead it kept them lashed together like a pair of Indian knife fighters, each trying to be the first to rip out the other's guts.[8]

The first shot in the war was fired not at the lab but over in marketing. Kassar wanted Laurel to develop a market for all the *Pac-Man* spinoffs that would soon be emerging from the lab, staffed as it was with all those nice obedient programmers. He had ordered *Ms. Pac-Man* before the lab got going, and the game was now nearly finished; in the works were things with names like *Son of Pac-Man* and *Pac-Man Three.* Management was hot to get game software into the Home Computer Division, because prior to *Pac-Man* exactly what a home computer was going to do was still a mystery. People bought them, played with them for a while, and eventually tossed them into the closet. Maybe things like *Pac-Man* would boost the sales of hardware to match that of software. Meanwhile the Atari game division continued to grind out riches as if it were grinding salt.

In the midst of this numbing plethora of sheer unencumbered wealth the mindless machinery of corporate profitability ground inexorably onward. Upper management scrutinized division reports with a no-sparrow-shall-fall mentality, and the slightest sign of lagging profits meant the Divine Hand of Retribution. In practice this policy meant that every week or two another marketing VP was shot out of the saddle. "They aren't happy with the biggest golden eggs anybody's ever seen," Dunion said. "They want the whole fucking goose." Inevitably, one day the shots hit Laurel. Although she was in marketing, Kay knew about her work, and they had been discussing a possible relationship with the lab for her at some future time. When she got her pink slip she immediately called Kay. Fortunately, he was in town. "Help!" Laurel said, with unaccustomed brevity.

Kay had her packed up, out of her office in marketing, and over to the lab in the same day. For both Laurel and Kay, the challenge of blue-sky research at the cutting edge of interactivity was what they'd come to Atari for, and it was time to put Laurel's pearls-before-swine sojourn in marketing behind them. When Ray Kassar found out she hadn't actually left the company, he sent a succession of unpleasant memos to Kay—all told, four of them—advising him of her inadequacies in ungentle terms. "This person is a *programmer*," Kassar fumed. Kay responded with sarcastic memos (which he tore up after ruminating over them) and polite memos (which he sent).

Laurel had wanted to do interactivity research in the first place, and she came to the task chock-full of ideas. But she found herself facing the same misunderstandings over the word *interactivity* that had shaped up over the word *research*. To Laurel, and to the rest of the lab, *interactivity* meant something like Andy Lippman's description back at MIT: "Mutual and simultaneous activity on the part of both participants, usually working toward some goal, but not necessarily."

Lippman enumerated five corollaries to his definition. One is *inter-ruptibility,* which means that each participant must be able to inter-rupt the other, mutually and simultaneously. The second is *graceful degradation,* which means that unanswerable questions must be han-dled in a way that doesn't halt the conversation: "I'll come back to that in a minute," for example. The third is *limited look-ahead,* which means that because both parties can be interrupted there is a limit to how much of the shape of the conversation can be anticipated by either party. The fourth is *no-default,* which means that the conversa-tion must not have a preplanned path, it must truly develop in the interaction. The fifth is that the participants must have *the impression of an infinite database,* which is to say that an immersive world should give the illusion of not being much more limiting in the choices it offers than an actual world would be.[9] Interactivity implied two conscious agencies in conversation, spontaneously developing a mu-tual discourse, taking cues and suggestions from each other on the fly. Laurel had added the additional elements of drama—interaction based on principles of stagecraft—and of ludics, playful interaction.

On the other hand, to the Atari management interactivity meant something quite different. Nobody had thought it out; if you stopped people and asked them, they said it was intuitively obvious. Inter-activity meant turn-taking, not interruption; it meant that the user pushed a button and the machine did something as a result. That process was interactive because the machine responded to the user's command, instead of doing something on its own. It was what Jim Dunion called poke-and-see technology. Many of the lab people felt that way about Apple's Hypercard—from the standpoint of interacti-vity it was a deception, because although it was a huge step forward in the popular dissemination of hypertext tools, it gave a facile illu-sion of what interactivity was.

The clash over interactivity shaped up as nastily as the one over research. Laurel got to fire one of the opening salvos quite uninten-tionally. Bob Stein, Kay's consultant, was working on an interactive encyclopedia with the Encyclopaedia Britannica company. Knowing

Laurel's interests, he had taken her on board the project. His liaison with the company was Charles Van Doren, the first contestant to be caught and convicted of cheating on the television quiz show "The $64,000 Question." The interactive encyclopedia let the user enter words for the program to look up. As far as Van Doren was concerned, in that fact inhered its interactivity. He came by Laurel's new office in the lab one day and proceeded to chat her up about interactivity. Laurel's ears perked up. "That's great," she said, "I'm working on interactivity too."

"You are?" Van Doren said.

"Sure," Laurel said enthusiastically. "I've got this idea for an interactive educational thing about whales told from multiple perspectives—whales from an Inuit perspective and then whales from a whaling corporation perspective and a Greenpeace perspective, say. Multiple narrative thread, user selectable. It'd fit right into your interactive encyclopedia."

Van Doren turned red and began to make a peculiar noise. After a few seconds Laurel realized he was sputtering. Finally he burst into speech. "Encyclopedias don't present *viewpoints*," he said, biting off the words. "Encyclopedias present *truth*."[10]

Sooner or later any discussion of interaction and how it works turned to debates over how to handle very large databases. After a database exceeds a certain size, it becomes impractical for a human to search even the major listings in a reasonably short period of time. Thus the fact of a database that contains, in the ideal case, all the knowledge of humankind, doesn't imply that such a database is searchable. This surprising fact was encountered in practice with the first large publicly searchable computerized databases in the 1960s. One of the first of these was the MEDLARS medical database, maintained at the National Institutes of Health in Bethesda, Maryland, for the National Library of Medicine. The MEDLARS database ran on a mainframe with access available only from a single console. There were no public terminals. Researchers wanting to use the database submitted requests for information on slips of paper, just as if they were requesting a book from the closed stacks. The library staff transcribed these requests onto standard forms and typed them into the console keyboard by hand. The answers came back a day or two later in the form of printouts from an IBM line printer.

Things did not proceed as expected. Researchers inquiring after information found to their dismay that a request for a list of titles of papers on a particular disease or drug might result in hundreds of feet of dense printout. Notices went up in the MEDLARS area warning people to be extremely cautious about how they worded their requests for information. Still the piles of paper proliferated. The reason was simple—there were simply too many data on each subject for the existing search protocols to handle. Key-word searches, the common method, simply did not work with so many data, because several thousand abstracts might share the same key words. Buried in the abstracts themselves was critical information by which they could be separated, but even programs that searched the abstracts themselves for key words or phrases found too much. Some different approach was needed.

The most advanced thinking about this problem was not about search protocols but about the abstract idea of searching and the ways that searching was done not in computers but in actual interaction with humans. The ideal model of a search device already existed. It was called a graduate student. Computer programmers tended to be so focused on mathematically derived search algorithms such as binary tree protocols and bubble sorts that the significance of the graduate student tended to escape them. Graduate students or research assistants make the best search devices because in ideal circumstances they become attuned to their professors' work and are able to gather just the kinds of information that fit the research project, beyond the capabilities of lists of authors or key words to capture the essence of the work. They take initiative, understand abstractions, and pursue corollary threads. At least the best of them do. This was precisely the kind of search device that a database such as MEDLARS required.

The people at the Atari Lab and the Media Lab called such devices, in their abstracted form, agents. How to produce such an agent has been an ongoing debate ever since the Media Lab researchers first sketched out the idea. In the 1980s, John Scully ordered a demo of Apple's dream machine for the 1990s, which the public relations division called the Knowledge Navigator. The device incorporated a phone, modem, E-mail, calendar, and voice-operated word processor. The most striking thing about the Knowledge Navigator was its interface. It used not the desktop metaphor but an agent metaphor. In the upper left-hand corner of the Navigator's screen was the image of a secretary-like person. The image looked like a video of a live male secretary, complete with a perky bow tie. (Apple's design team had wanted to avoid the stereotype of a woman in the secretarial position, which left them with the only gender alternative available to a large mainstream corporation. The bow tie was an attempt to demasculinize the agent.) "Humans naturally talk to humans," Dunion would say, waving his arms. "Humans don't naturally talk to computers. We've spent millions of years learning how to talk to each other. Why change now?"

Talking to a program that is written to look like a human implies some things about interaction. The main one is that the program is convincing enough to actually engage the human—that the program possesses a depth and complexity that make the interaction convincing. Somewhere between talking to a cartoon face that answers in a mechanical monotone and talking to a photo-quality image that expresses the full gamut of human emotions lies the treacherous ground of agent experimentation, and it goes on at full speed today. When Laurel raised the first questions about dramatic interaction, she implied the computer as actor, which led to the same problems vis-à-vis agents: How could characters on the computer screen be created that were convincing?

Central to the construction of agents was the idea of *presence*. What, exactly, was it about a representation that gave it the illusion of personal force, of a living being? And conversely, what did it take to convince a person by means of a representation of a place that they were actually present *in* that place? The Atari Lab researchers talked about it long and often. Just what was presence, really, they asked; and how do we manipulate it?

It seemed obvious that talking about presence wasn't going to be enough. They had to experiment with presence, to play with the concept of agency in practical situations. In the middle of these discussions they more or less stumbled on the construct that they came to call Arthur Fischell.

Arthur was at first a purely conceptual person, a thought experiment in what it took to make an artificial persona seem real. What went into creating a believable virtual agent, really? The original idea came from Susan Brennan. For a while he was known simply as Arthur, and then Brennan exercised creator's privilege and gave him a last name. Thus his origins were covertly expressed in his name— Arti-ficial. Later he also acquired a wife named Olivia. Arthur and Olivia Fischell, the team chuckled. If they wanted believability in their agents, how better to start?[11]

The team thought of Arthur as another member of the lab. (Olivia was a homemaker, so she avoided the hard parts of the experiment.) They set out to explore how his sense of presence could be developed and how it needed to be tweaked in order to create an aura of reality for him. At first his persona was honored more by reference than by his own speech, like the legendary Kilroy. People talked about him, rather than Arthur himself doing any talking. Shortly it became clear that just talking about him in the third person was too limiting, and Arthur would have to start doing some talking of his own. Since he didn't exist in the physical sense, this requirement presented some problems; but many of the lab's day-to-day interactions already occurred via E-mail, and the team seized on this fact for their first experiment. Thus Arthur's personality developed and flourished at first entirely on E-mail, where the problem of voice could be ignored. Various lab people who were privy worked on his character—Jim Dunion, Michael Naimark, Ann Marion, Brenda Laurel, Eric

Hulteen, and Susan Brennan were in on the experiment and each could log on as Arthur. They added to his persona in a deliberate way from time to time, but after a while he began to grow on his own, by a kind of accretion. Perhaps his own embryonic personality was beginning to assert its presence.

People at the lab frequently put on-line brief résumés and statements of what their research interests were. These were kept in special files called finger files, which anyone could read by "fingering" the individual's name. After a while the Arthur team put on-line an elaborate and quirkily humorous résumé of Arthur's achievements in a finger file of his own—he'd invented squid jerky, for example, and made significant contributions to the development of muffler bearings, and before coming to Atari he'd had a distinguished career with the British Postal Service. The team was still only half serious, playing around with ideas of identity without much sense of where they were going, and unconsciously they were creating Arthur as a kind of liminal character. He had some quotidian attributes, and also some that were obviously whimsical. But as it turned out, his persona would become so overwhelmingly real that the whimsical attributes would come to be overlooked, or astonishingly misread so as to make them fit into an acceptable image of a genuine, if eccentric, person.

It was now early 1983, and Alan Kay had begun dropping hints about needing more assistants. Kay was gone much of the time doing other things, such as attending corporate meetings and traveling the lecture circuit, and his absence was being noticed . . . and decisions about the lab needed to be made day by day. Kay's regular guy and heir apparent to the title of director pro tem was Mike Liebhold, whose claim to fame was that he specialized in big databases. But by this time the interesting work at the lab wasn't being done in database construction; it was being done by the people working with problems of agency, dramatic interaction, and presence. In the meantime Arthur Fischell had been gaining reality points as the team continued to work away at building his character. Kay was following the Arthur experiment with interest, so one day, by fiat, he decided to kick it along. He published a memo to the company at large announcing that in his absence Arthur would be pro tem director of the lab.

Arthur responded to his new authority by blossoming into a much more distinctive and complex personality. He became known around Atari as a suave, intelligent, smooth-spoken guy, mature and sexy, slightly rakish in a Victorian way—in fact, rather noticeably like the personality of Nick Negroponte, the lab's godfather. The resemblance was probably not happenstance. Arthur acquired a corner office, furnished in typically Arthurian idiosyncratic fashion. For example, Scott Fisher had found an old airline seat and brought it in to the lab, with the idea of eventually using it for an experiment. In the meantime the team borrowed it and installed it in Arthur's office; where, it was said, he used it instead of a desk chair. The sight of the thing behind Arthur's desk seemed in keeping with Arthur's quirky personality.

Of course, Arthur was almost never in town either, being always off on some mission or other of his own just like Alan Kay. But unlike Kay, he was extremely active on E-mail, keeping up a continuous flow of conversation and bombarding people with questions about the progress of their experiments.

In and around the lab there were the beginnings of the fights between lab folk and the systems engineering people, border skirmishes that would later blossom into a full-scale war. Systems folks thought the MIT crew to be, in their words, effete little pricks. The systems engineers were what lab folk called pocket protector people, and in the term could be understood the magnitude of the culture clash that was shaping up. Battles of words began to rage on interoffice E-mail between the groups, and in these clashes Arthur was always the cool voice of moderation. After a while, the Arthur team noticed that there was an occasional piece of mail from someone in engineering or sales, asking for Arthur's advice on some intradepartmental disagreement. Apparently people in other departments were hearing about this Solomonesque person in the lab and were seeking out his opinion. The team fed this tiny flame of belief assiduously. They spent hours talking about ways to ramp up Arthur's reality controls. Finally digital music technology provided an unexpected breakthrough. One day Jim Dunion showed up with an Eventide Harmonizer, a device that changes the pitch of any sound that passes through it. The team took one look at the Harmonizer and decided that it was time for Arthur to have a real voice. Laurie Anderson was already using a Harmonizer to change the pitch of her voice in live performance, but the team didn't know that. Mara set the device up and practiced with it, getting used to how it worked and what its limits were. Finally the team decided to give the Arthurian vocal presence a test run. They hooked the Harmonizer up to a speakerphone and took out their notepads. Laurel dialed up the MIS office—and accidentally got connected to the senior vice president of Atari.

Everyone in the room snapped to full attention. "What do I do now?" Laurel mouthed silently. "Keep going," Ann Marion mouthed back. So while the team listened, gripping their notepads, Laurel bulled ahead. Speaking as Arthur, with the deep voice of the Eventide Harmonizer, she wound up convincing the VP that Arthur was in Boston on important business. Arthur left a phone number in the event that Atari needed to reach him. Laurel was completely unbriefed as to how to carry the masquerade to that extreme, and in the background the team scrabbled around for a plausible Boston phone number. Finally they came up with a number that Laurel fed to the VP. Then she hung up, astonished by the extent of the masquerade. She looked around at the team, and Scott Fisher said, "I hope he doesn't actually try that number. He'll wind up talking to Boston Dial-a-Prayer."

The team realized that something quite interesting was going on. The experiment in presence was succeeding beyond anything they'd anticipated. They had actually convinced a significant part of the Atari Corporation that a person named Arthur Fischell existed, and further, that he was acting director of the lab. Insidiously they had even been winning over some lab members. But the greater population of the lab wasn't convinced. "Muffler bearings," some snorted.

Shortly they challenged Arthur to either appear in person, or, failing that, to hold a live teleconference with the company at large from wherever he happened to be.

The Arthur team took up the challenge. They couldn't handle a personal appearance, but a teleconference was just enough within reach to be truly daunting. They raced around the company, grabbing audio and video equipment wherever they could find it. They came in the next weekend when the lab was deserted and spent 48 frantic hours cabling the place. They ran audio and video feeds out of the lab area, hiding the cables behind the overhead tiling. In a remote part of the building they threw together a makeshift video studio, complete with lighting and sets. They'd succeeded in creating an E-mail presence; then they'd created a vocal presence; now they were about to stage the debut of Arthur's visual presence.

What did Arthur look like, really? The team held a strategy meeting, and decided that he might as well look like Brenda Laurel. Laurel would play Arthur for the live cameras. That bracketed his appearance; it gave him some limits with regard to size, height, build, and so forth. On the day of the teleconference the team sneaked away to the hidden studio and spent four hours prepping for the performance. Brenda needed makeup to create the visual Arthur, and the Eventide Harmonizer to create his voice. She and Jim Dunion were about the same size, so she borrowed some of his clothing. She did a careful makeup job—gray temples, crepe hair sideburns, moustache, and a hat to cover the abundant blond hair on her head. Dunion hooked the Harmonizer up between Brenda's microphone and the audio feed to the conference room.

The conference was set up to be two-way, with live questions and answers from the audience. In the audience was Douglas Adams, author of *The Hitchhiker's Guide to the Galaxy,* who was visiting the lab that day to give a talk of his own.

At Zero Hour the screen in the lab's spacious conference room lit up to show the elusive Arthur Fischell calmly seated behind his desk. He made a few opening remarks, a sort of State-of-the-Lab Address in miniature, and then threw the meeting open for questions from the live audience in the conference room. People asked questions about how the company was doing, whether there were any new plans for the lab, and so forth. Arthur answered with his accustomed rakish aplomb, occasionally rising to pace the room or to sit on the edge of his desk. During his answers the video switchers interspersed shots of him with prepared charts and graphs. And because the team couldn't leave well enough alone, they had built the set to include several windows behind which were landscapes. The landscapes came from an assortment of travel posters that Scott Fisher had cut up, but no two posters were of the same country. During the cutaway shots to the graphs while he was not on camera, Arthur shifted position from one window to another, thus giving the effect (to the alert viewer) of being in one country in one shot and then suddenly in another one for the next. This sort of thing produced much giggling in the control room.

Then Arthur pulled one of his extravagant moves. Wanda Royce, a member of the research team, had once been Miss North Dakota, although she had not mentioned the fact to anyone at Atari. None of the lab people knew either, but now Arthur nonchalantly waved his hand, and boom—the screen filled with Wanda coming down the ramp in the Miss North Dakota pageant, many years before. It was Arthur's way of demonstrating his omniscience and power, by instantly and offhandedly being able to produce an obscure item of someone's personal history. In reality, the team had scrambled to acquire the tape from the network at a very high price.

The audience was suitably impressed.

Insofar as the conference was a test of whether Arthur could convince an audience that he was real, it was an unqualified success. Muffler bearings in his résumé notwithstanding, the percentage of people at Atari who believed in him had risen to near 100 percent. But there were unexpected side effects. The most striking was that some people remained unconvinced not of Arthur's reality, but instead they were unconvinced that the conference had been live and interactive. After all, they reasoned, the focus of much of the lab's work was on interactivity, and the conference was a golden opportunity to test out some of the things they'd been finding out. They believed that Arthur had been recorded some time before the "live" conference, and that what they had seen had been a playback of portions of the recording, cued by some sort of voice recognition system. Arthur's seeming to answer questions from the audience had been a trick of some very slick programming. The cuts between segments that were necessary with such a system had been made invisible by the programmers' hacking the switching gear. That, they felt, had been the whole purpose of the Arthur deception.

Laurel, peeling off her crepe sideburns, shook her head in amazement. "Jeez," she said, "he's real, but he's not live. Just the opposite of what we'd expected."

The Arthur team decided it was a good lesson. "I think we learned more about presence from the conference than from anything else we did," Fisher said. "It's been very interesting, how you construct the illusion of a person." Afterward Laurel, Susan Brennan, Adam Laurent, and Alan Kay went to Ray Kassar's private dining room to have lunch with Douglas Adams. During lunch, Adams noticed a tiny flake of spirit gum adhering to Laurel's cheek. He lifted an eyebrow, smiled, and said, "So you're the one . . ."

On occasion, being in the closet about her work on Arthur had negative consequences for Laurel. Some time during 1982 the company provided new offices for the entire lab staff. Laurel went to her office and found another researcher occupying it. A heated exchange ensued, during which the newcomer sat tight. He gave the clear impression that he didn't give a shit whether the office had been assigned to Laurel; in his opinion Laurel wasn't a researcher, she was some kind of hanger-on, and she shouldn't have had an office. At any rate he was there and he intended to stay. She tried reason, then she tried cajoling, and finally ended up screaming at him. Nothing worked.

Laurel wound up storming the Old Man's office. "Look, am I a researcher, or not?" she asked.

"Of course you are," Kay responded.

Laurel snapped back, "If I'm a researcher, then get that mother-fucker out of my office."

Finally Kay stepped in and got the interloper out, but the event was symptomatic. Aside from Nick Negroponte's original and enlightened encouragement to hire as many women as possible, Ann Marion, Susan Brennan, and the other women in the lab maintained their positions by virtue of possessing commonly intelligible technical skills. Without those skills they were still second-class citizens. With the skills, they occupied a special category, which the anthropologist Barbara Joans calls "dancing dogs." Since Laurel's skills were unintelligible, when the men weren't consciously on their best behavior she still found herself being treated as second class. By now she was stressed anyway, feeling that she was being looked down on by lab people who didn't like her credentials and didn't understand what she was doing. Unlike people at the administrative level, her peers at the lab tended to treat her as a person with great potential but not much knowledge. This attitude was manifested in such ways as what came to be called the SIGGRAPH '83 Shutout. When SIGGRAPH time came around, as was customary, the lab sent all its people out to Anaheim for the show . . . except for Laurel, who became the only person singled out not to attend. The office rumor mill had it that going to SIGGRAPH wouldn't be useful for her.

Laurel went to Kay and asked him what was going on. Kay looked thoughtful, and then said he didn't believe it was useful for anyone to attend SIGGRAPH if they didn't know how to program a computer. He gave her a book on graphic programming. Laurel grimaced, and added, "This is the best indicator I've seen of the lab's state of mind. Why should you need to program in order to understand graphics?" Then she asked what Kay was doing to promote interest among the lab staff in how entertainment worked. Nothing, Kay responded; they were designing computers, not entertainment.

Laurel responded by making a pitch for the importance of understanding how entertainment worked if the lab intended to make entertainment products. After all, she pointed out, Atari was one of the world's largest manufacturers of entertainment software . . . *entertainment* software, not merely programs. She pointed out that almost without exception the lab staff had immense experience with hardware and software, but virtually no experience at all with what people did with it. Finally she reasoned, cajoled, and bullied Kay into sending the lab staff to Disney's Epcot Center in Orlando for an educational tour, pointing out that the world's largest entertainment software company should learn something from the world's largest entertainment company.

After a while Kay agreed. (Evidently he took this lesson to heart, judging by later interviews in which he talks about the importance of learning environments.) Laurel proceeded to arrange the tour to coincide with a space shuttle launch. Later, several lab people would say that the Epcot tour was useful, but that watching the shuttle launch had approached a religious experience—it had profoundly and permanently affected their lives.

Although the team didn't know it, the end of the lab was approaching too quickly for them to exploit the things they'd learned from Arthur, from Disney, and from the interaction research they'd then barely begun.

The game software market finally peaked around 1982, and after that time revenues began slowly to drop. It didn't matter that they were dropping in relation to the most profitable financial situation that any American company had ever enjoyed; by the relentless logic of business, the romance had now gone sour. There was also something awry with the books, but that fact wouldn't become clear for another year or two. Atari immediately started layoffs. In some areas of the company these were fairly serious as early as 1983, but by 1984 rumors were beginning to circulate that layoff fever might reach as far down as the lab. Management had to make decisions about whether the direction the company intended to pursue was going to be only making product for the current market or also doing development for potential markets. Ted Hoff, Atari's newest VP and the person directing most of the layoffs, believed that Atari's future lay not in interactivity—which, as was becoming clear, the company as a whole understood not at all—but in hardware, specifically in VLSI (very large scale integrated circuit) technology. A VLSI chip is a specialized component incorporating a microprocessor, some memory, and a permanent program all together on a single chip. The chip runs only the program for which it was designed, and it can be made extremely small because it doesn't need the frequently bulky general-purpose components that a personal computer must have in order to properly run whatever software happens to be loaded into it. Products like Gameboy are based on specialized VLSI chips rather than generic chips running external programs.

Atari had a VLSI department of its own that was separate from the lab. The VLSI people didn't do research; they worked from a set of accepted design principles to produce custom special-purpose chips. It was a craft job, requiring set kinds of skills. The chips ran programs that were written by the game division; thus the lab wasn't in the VLSI loop at all. Hoff, who oversaw both divisions, wasn't particularly happy with the lab. He tended to treat the lab and its staff like an exotic tropical bird with an extremely low IQ. It was nice to look at, but didn't do much of anything useful. Hoff didn't care about research. Research, he felt, was tomorrow. Today he had a bottom line to meet, and the hell with tomorrow; he wanted product, not speculation.

Hoff was representative of the entire management philosophy at Atari. From the beginning, and continuing as the company exploded in size, upper management had continued to recruit the middle management corps from places like Procter and Gamble, Lever Brothers, and Clorox . . . good, solid people with little imagination who had solid track records as business managers. It was said that none of them had had computers in their offices at their former companies, and none had computers in their offices at Atari. They weren't embarrassed to say that personal computers were merely a passing fad, and that after all the excitement died away Atari would have done its consumer research and would get on with producing whatever the merchandise was for the next fad.

Patently life under this dispensation was not an atmosphere conducive to starry-eyed romanticizing about the future of technology. With the attention of higher management palpably turning to immediate results, the members of the lab found themselves in the position of having been hired to perform a series of tasks that management was now indicating it felt were odious. There was no doubt that they were pushing the envelope of long-term agent research, but Atari's support for the lab was quickly evaporating; under the new and stricter policies the lab *had no* short-term mandate.

In addition, they were beginning to experience the downside effects of one of the very things the lab had been organized to exploit: the results of continual culture clash between the long-range researchers and the medium-range manufacturers, with the added red herring of the short-range profiteers thrown in. Kay's (and Negroponte's, had he been present) original idea behind throwing these groups together had been productive clashes, cross-fertilizations. Because of, or perhaps in spite of, Kay's prolonged absences, the cross-fertilization wasn't occurring. In fact, the pattern that was rapidly emerging was quite the opposite—continual suspicion on the part of the manufacturers and outright contempt on the part of the profiteers.

Part of the reason for these reactions might have been the deliberately blurry lines between the young technoturks in the lab and the postadolescent terrors down the hall who played at computer games in the guise of work. From a distance they were more or less indistinguishable. That similarity had been okay when the tiny terrors were practically spouting cash from their fingertips, cash enough to float the entire corporate vessel with enough left over to enrich anyone who came close. But that was then, and this was now. The bloom was off the kids. Their tiny imperfections, always noticeable but easy to ignore in the golden haze of enormous profitability, now stood out like mountains on the moon. What were they doing, management began to ask, besides playing around?

Sensing impending trouble, the lab staff held a series of internal meetings. The idea had something to do with a combination of self-promotion and self-policing. Kay, as usual, was off somewhere, and Arthur couldn't handle a job that required extensive face-to-face interaction. The staff met anyway, and with Kay's (and Arthur's) concurrence they elected Christina Hooper, one of the original MIT group, as acting manager. Hooper instituted a system of technical reports, and then forgot to sign off on them. But before this could become a problem, Kay came back and called a special meeting.

The situation at Atari at this moment, of which Kay was either unaware or pretending to be unaware, was this: One of Atari's New York executives had been caught with his hand deep in the cookie jar. The books had been rigged to cover the losses, which were considerable. This deception might not have been noticed or cared about, as in the past, except for one new and unheralded thing: *All* the new Atari games—taken together, the most valuable and potentially the most lucrative licensing agreement in the history of game software—had turned out to be disasters.

This fact should not have been surprising, really. Atari felt that it was finally able to closely supervise and control game production, and thus to bring order to an unruly business by imposing customary, sensible merchandising standards and marketing techniques. To this end they secured the rights to produce games based on two blockbuster films: *Superman* and *E.T.* Both games were to be designed and written under the philosophy that they were, first and foremost, *products.* No wild-eyed shredders would determine their content. They would be aimed at what management saw as an even larger market: the "family." They would be good, wholesome products, and they would walk off the shelves just as quickly as *E.T.* lunch boxes and action figures.

Thus Atari was finally manufacturing product written under a corporate philosophy that was virtually (some lab folk would add "willfully") ignorant of what went into writing successful interactive games. The projects were being supervised by middle managers who were proud of the fact that they'd never touched computers and by fortysomething NASA hands who were used to carrying slide rules. They had learned to drive Mercedes and to dress like the smooth New York executives whose helicopters regularly landed in Atari's parking lot, but there was little of the spark of imagination in them. They were, after all, accustomed to government projects that took four or five years to complete and for which the most important creative factor was that revision orders be filed in numerical order.

The *Superman* and *E.T.* games arrived at the dealers—and sat on the shelves as if they were bolted down.

In other circumstances they might still have moved out of the stores strictly on Atari's reputation, but as it turned out, the final thing that Kassar and the other Atari top managers had failed to understand was the speed of information on the street. By the time the new games hit the shelves, word was already out in the tight-knit and fanatically attentive gaming communities that *Superman* and *E.T.–The Game* were terrible. Suddenly the thousands of former Atari gamers found new and engrossing pastimes elsewhere, while the family market, whatever that was, simply failed to materialize. And a new and unheralded thing began to happen at Atari's shipping division: returns began to come in. First there was a trickle of them—most retailers couldn't believe it either, and waited for the games to move as they always had—but shortly they woke up and smelled the cappuccino, and the trickle of returns turned into a cataract.

Almost immediately Atari's stock began to plummet.

At the lab meeting, either Kay didn't know about these things or chose not to mention them; at any rate, he was running on a tape of his own, a reaction to the earlier gloomy financial picture. He was growing uncomfortably aware that the gulf between the lab and the rest of the company, not particularly dangerous in the palmy days, could easily prove fatal in Atari's current financial straits. What he did do was talk about who was hiring in the rest of the industry.

There they were in the middle of another interminable lab meeting, and all of a sudden Kay was talking about other job opportunities.

It was so bizarre and unexpected that many people didn't even notice he'd done it until after the meeting had ended; the blissful bubble of invulnerability that surrounded the lab was hard to breach. "Did you notice?" Eric Hulteen asked later. "Alan was talking about job openings at *DARPA!* Now why the hell would he do that?"

They found out a few days later. At 8 A.M., the top brass called Christina Hooper in and told her to fire 20 to 30 percent of the lab staff immediately. The first anyone in the lab knew about it was when Hooper came into John McClelland's office, sat on the edge of his desk, and said, "I need your badge."

"Huh?" McClelland said.

"I need your badge. You're fired. You have five minutes to get your stuff together." She paused, then added in a lower voice, "I'm sorry."

McClelland just sat there, with his mouth hanging open, and a guard walked in, carrying a cardboard box. Hooper took McClelland's badge, stood up, and went on to the next office. McClelland dazedly began filling the box with his personal stuff. Then Hooper started in on the core people, the best and the brightest whom Alan Kay had romanced personally—Laurel, Fisher, Hulteen, and nine or ten others. In a few hours Hooper had cleared out around 20 people. "It came as a complete shock," Fisher said bitterly. "One afternoon it was 'Here's our plan for the next 15 years, here's 15 million bucks, let's get busy,' and the next morning it was 'Can you have your things packed and be out of your office in 15 minutes?'"

A few days later they did it again. In two or three waves of firing, the population of the lab dwindled by half.

While the firings were going on, Atari's stock dropped through the floor, and it was still dropping. On top of the sinking game market, news of how Atari had been looted from within had badly shaken investors, who were now operating in dump mode. Living only in the present, Time Warner was frantically searching for someone to take this losing prospect off their hands. They found their angel in the person of Jack Tramiel, who had piloted a nearby computer company in the valley until a stockholders' rebellion had ousted him.

Tramiel had the reputation of being the baddest, meanest manager in the computer business; those who had worked under him were fond of referring to him as Jabba the Hutt.[12] "The mildest thing anybody said about him," Dunion related, "was that he was a vicious, coldhearted, bloodthirsty shark." Tramiel had survived prison camps during World War II and wasn't going to let Silicon Valley slow him up one bit. He bought Atari from Warner for what amounted to salvage costs. Once he had hold of Atari, word came down that he was preparing to clear everybody out and move his team in. Normally this process takes a while, but not when you are hungry, in a hurry to cut costs to nothing, and utterly ruthless.

The scene at the Silicon Valley complex was reminiscent of the last hours of the U.S. Embassy in Saigon. At 8 A.M. word had arrived that Tramiel had taken over and that his goons were coming to clear the buildings. *Everybody* was fired. Hooper communicated it to the remaining lab people by announcing, "Jabba the Hutt is on his way." While Tramiel and his goons were on their way—for all anybody knew, in armored assault vehicles—Warner's guards were already conducting sweeps of the buildings, clearing everyone out, and boxing up whatever was abandoned in the process. The mood shifted to full-scale panic. People who had just discovered what was happening were frantically trying to collect their personal belongings. Others on the upper floors opened their windows and began dropping things out—into the bushes if they were lucky, onto the pavement if they weren't, occasionally into the open trunks of their cars parked at the curb—things like chairs, bookcases, sofas, stereo systems, and television sets. Occasionally a TV exploded on impact, sending a gout of dust and debris spouting upward from the trunk, and kicking the trunk lid into seesawing madly in the aftershock. Guards were herding secretaries and lower-echelon workers into the street like farm animals, some bewildered, some in tears.

Amid the confusion, scurrying, shouting, and occasional screams, Larry Bowles sauntered in the front entrance, walked up to the security guard with a comb wrapped in a wad of tissue paper, and said, "I need an equipment pass for this personal item I'm taking inside."

"What is it?" the guard asked, pulling out the form.

"It's a Dynair switcher," Bowles said, naming an extremely expensive, high-end piece of video gear.

"Okay," the guard said, writing out the pass.

An hour or so later Bowles came back downstairs lugging a huge, expensive, top-of-the-line Dynair video switcher, went to the door, and handed the guard the pass. "One Dynair switcher," the guard said. "Personal property. Thank you." Bowles put it in his car and drove away.

Dunion and Gano took refuge on the upper floors, perhaps in hope of a rescue helicopter. Somehow the guards missed them during the next-to-final sweep. The two of them walked slowly downstairs, through the empty, echoing hallways drifted with debris, and into the silent, blue-lit warehouse, which was already filling up with rows of cardboard boxes stuffed with personal items the guards had collected. They turned and went back into the lab building, and walked upstairs to Hoff's old office. The building was shockingly empty, its suddenly abandoned spaces surreal. Drifts of discarded files littered the floors. It reminded Gano of the Hall of Records in *Orfeo Negro*. They sat there in the deserted building, soaking it up.

At about 9:30, Tramiel's goons evicted the Warner troops and conducted their own sweep. This time they found Dunion and Gano in Hoff's office. The office was higher than the adjoining building, and although the day was gray the spacious windows made the bare, stripped room appear light and cheerful. There was the sound of boots in the hall, and suddenly a Tramiel shock trooper loomed in the doorway. "You leave now," he said, eloquently.

"Now?" Gano said. "We still have to pack up these tapes." He indicated a stack of Dunion's personal videotapes.

"Okay, but nothing that says Atari on it," the guard said.

All Dunion's tapes said Atari on the boxes . . . until recently it had been something of a mark of pride. So Dunion and Gano took turns, one of them distracting the guard while the other surreptitiously dropped the tapes, one at a time, out the window. As they were completing this operation, there were more footsteps in the hall, and a young, fresh-faced, friendly kid in Tramiel livery came in. "Hi!" he said. "What are you guys doin'?"

Dunion and Gano looked at each other, then at the kid. "Packing up," Gano said. "And you?"

"I'm part of the Atari research team," the kid said. "Jack Tramiel just hired us. It's really exciting. We're going to start an Atari research lab. We're going to do blue-sky research here. Tramiel says there'll be no limit to what we can do. Cutting-edge stuff!"

Dunion and Gano just goggled at him. After a minute, Gano intoned, in a sepulchral voice, "Welcome . . . to the Twilight Zone."

Some time later, kids riding their bikes in New Mexico discovered some plastic things that looked like computer cartridges sticking out of a landfill. Atari's shipping department, it seems, had been shipping hundreds of thousands of *Superman* and *E.T.* cartridges—not to dealers, but to be buried somewhere where, hopefully, they would never be found.

Segue to Austin, Texas, March 1993

7

The End of Innocence, Part II: Cyberdämmerung at Wellspring Systems

At the edge of a small Midwestern city noted for its high-tech industries sits a sleek new office complex, complete with indoor atrium featuring a twenty-foot waterfall. Inside nestle the corporate headquarters of Wellspring Systems. The company's generous office windows overlook a nature conservation area not far from the company's door, complete with dense, deep green foliage and brilliantly plumed exotic birds. Wellspring is an extremely successful computer game company, one of the first to produce a widely popular game. It has followed up on this with a succession of popular programs based more or less on the same theme: shoot-'em-up games filled with intense action, high-tech war machinery, and conventionally beautiful women whose purpose is to be sexually available to the protagonist's gaze. In the programmers' lair, which at Wellspring is a long, claustrophobic hallway lined with narrow doors, life goes on as it has at game companies since the palmy days at the Atari Game Division, back in Silicon Valley in the mid-eighties.

But there are notable differences. Gone is the freewheeling, anything-goes atmosphere, gone the enormous sense of expectancy. Not that the work isn't exciting. The doors in the programmers' lair open on the same tiny cubicles, and the tokens of the technokid culture are still in evidence—here some crushed bags of Cheetos and a stack of empty Jolt cans, there a dirty, rumpled sleeping bag unrolled underneath a long table stacked with untidy piles of software. The differences are not immediately obvious, but include such basics as the distribution of wealth. The programmers' situation at Wellspring is far removed from that of the Atari programmers, who were pulling down sixty to eighty thousand dollars a year on royalties in the 1980s when eighty thousand was a fair amount of money. Instead, the Wellspring kids work on fixed salaries, not royalties, and in the back of their eyes lurks fear—fear of getting old without having hit the jackpot with a runaway selling program: that is, fear of turning 30. And fear of the hundreds of technokids waiting outside for one of the elect to stumble, to falter, to make that tiny fatal error that magically turns them into one of the outsiders and lets another outsider in. Such fatal errors include objecting to the killingly long hours and low pay.

The owners of the digital sweatshop grimly enforce the pressure-cooker atmosphere of competition. They are multimillionaires. Sam Lerner drives to work in a Lamborghini Countach, a $150,000 ultra-high-performance sports car that gets 10 miles to the gallon. He is 32 years old.

Unlike the golden days of Silicon Valley, there isn't even a pretense of trickle-down economics in the new world of software games. When Wellspring was acquired by a major, well-established game company with main offices in Silicon Valley, there was a celebration at the offices, with cheap cake and soft drinks. During the ensuing congratulatory speeches, one of the programmers asked whether some of the enormous profits made by Lerner during the sale would be distributed in the form of bonuses. Lerner looked at him as if he were some new species of vermin, and said, "Of course not."

Nine years after the women at the Atari Lab first asked why there weren't more women in game programming, 100 percent of the programmers at Wellspring are male. There is a single woman associated with one of the development teams, though not as a programmer. Susan Macintosh is in her early forties, a dynamic, fiery dialogue writer who aspires to be a producer, which is the person who actually determines the shape and purpose of a game. Over the years she has written a series of intriguing game plots designed to interest players of both sexes in something more complex than shooting at enemy blips. She presents these as possible games, and the programmers routinely ignore them.

During a recent development session Macintosh finally convinced one of the staff producers to take on such a project. She'd been trying for three years. After the meeting she left on vacation for a week. She returned to find that the project had been scrapped. "Too complicated," her boss said. "We replaced it with a shoot-the-helicopter game."

Macintosh patiently pointed out that the helicopter game had no plot. Of course she was patient. If she hadn't been patient, if in fact she weren't possessed of the patience of a certified saint, three years of this would have sent her screaming whacko.

"That's okay," the producer said. "People don't want plot. They just want to shoot things."

Memphis Smith is a short man of medium build. A bit older than most of his charges on the programming team, he is in his early thirties; unlike them, he is highly fashion conscious in a Texan way, given to silk shirts, blousy pants, and silver-toed cowboy boots. He has shoulder-length jet black hair and a short black beard. Smith is a supervisor, in charge of an entire game production team. He has been with Wellspring from the very beginning, way back in the dark ages, in 1985. The game he is supervising is called *Battle Commander*, which promises to be the biggest seller in Wellspring's history.

During Wellspring's most recent new product rollout at Comdex in Las Vegas, the company debuted a prerelease version of *Battle Commander*. Comdex was Smith's finest hour. As the game's supervisor, he'd spent months honchoing his producer and pack of programmers along. He'd tracked and herded every facet of its development, and was now at the Wellspring booth, decked out in his customary silk shirt, receiving the plaudits of the throng. Nearby was his wife, keeping just out of the way. The brilliant arc lights in the vast vaulted ceiling glittered in the polished silver toes of his black Justin boots.

The opening screen for *Battle Commander* shows a naked young woman covered by a thin sheet, lying on an army cot. When the cursor passes over her, she sits up and looks seductively out at the player. Smith was particularly proud of this screen. At Comdex he was usually surrounded by a knot of chatting, admiring young men, and he hardly noticed that the few women who stopped to watch the demo shook their heads in disappointment or disgust and walked away.

The second morning of the Comdex show a woman from the marketing division of Electronic Arts went up to Smith and asked politely, "How might I go about influencing the way women are depicted in this game?"

Smith looked her over as if she were a putrefying fish. He inflated his chest just a bit—something of an accomplishment, considering his already cocky attitude. "Well, little lady," he said in an exaggerated drawl, "tell you what, why don't you just take it up with the artist, or better yet,"—he leaned in at her, pushing his face close to hers, his voice dripping sarcasm—"*Why don't you just call my boss and get me fired?*"

There was a pause. "I see," she said, and walked away.

"'The way women are depicted in the game,'" Smith chuckled. "You can always tell the ones that never get any."

His wife nodded in assent. She was perfectly coiffed and made up; she wears full makeup even when swimming. She was wearing the sort of dress that a wisecracking 1940s detective might have said was sprayed on. In her flawless makeup, perfectly arranged blond hair, high heels and improbably formfitting costume she bore a startling resemblance to Mattel's Barbie. In response to Smith's witticism she smiled, a bright, perfect, dazzling, crimson-lined Barbie smile. She agreed with him completely. It was a moment out of *The Stepford Wives*.

A few weeks after Comdex, Sam Lerner's phone rang at Wellspring headquarters. He grabbed the receiver and found himself on the line with Larry Pierce, president of the company that has just acquired a controlling share of Wellspring stock from him. Pierce was curt, and wasted no time on introductions.

"Change it," he said.

"Change what?" Lerner asked, puzzled.

"The loading screen on *Battle Commander*. Change it."

Lerner, who had things 100 percent his way since he started the company, said blandly, "I really think that's our decision to make, Larry. We designed the game, and we know the market."

"Change it."

Smith came roaring into Bomber Area, fists balled, boot heels pounding the carpet. The first person he saw was Chris Roberts, the brother of *Battle Commander*'s producer. Roberts was clearly startled to see Smith so enraged. He strode up to Roberts and snarled, "Larry says to change the opening screen!" Smith looked wildly around the bullpen, shoulder-length black hair whipping at his face. He reached up and pushed it back, the veins in his arm bulging around the gold band of his Rolex. "Somebody is trying to polarize this team. I know it's them damn frog women."

Frog women is Smith's term for women who do not meet his standard of attractiveness, which includes any woman with the temerity to remark on the quality of his games. "Them damn frog women don't like what we're doing. Stirring up trouble like that. Where do they come off saying *Battle Commander* is sexist?" He pounded his fist against the door. "There is *absolutely no sexism* in this game!"

He began to pace, the silver points of his boots kicking wads of paper out of the way. "Never. Never in hell. Never will we change this game for a bunch of flaming assholes!"

Roberts calmed him down. They decided on what they believed was a compromise. The naked woman stayed. A second cot appeared in the screen, on which lay a naked man, also covered with a sheet. He did not sit up when cursored.

Electronic Arts was one of the few game companies to evince a serious interest in what makes games salable to target groups other than adolescent boys. Trip Hawkins and Larry Probst, two of its principals, have given talks here and there on what their research has shown. "We don't want to change the world," Hawkins has said, "but we feel we can do a better job and still increase our market share. We've been doing some research into gender differences. This stuff is still in the beginning stage, but I can report on a little of it. For instance, we know you can get a boy to go out and kill and destroy (in a game) for the sake of his commander, or the president, or the country. Or maybe just because he feels like killing. In other words, boys will kill for the sake of an idea. But we also know that you can get a girl to go out and kill (in a game) to rescue a wounded child or a parent. In other words, boys kill for the sake of ideas, and girls kill for the sake of individuals."

Electronic Arts is researching a line of games for young women. And while the amount of publicity this activity has generated may be greater than the results have warranted, it is a small beginning but still a real one. Other, more exciting research by other organizations is unfortunately still secret as this article goes to press. Recently, however, another game software company seized on this information to begin researching a line of mindless, bang-bang-shoot-em-up games for girls.

There is a lot at stake for us in the Wellspring story, with its grim real-world look at what contemporary game programming is like. It points out that there is no mandate in our culture to do anything in particular with the powerful technologies we have at our command. Of course information technology in all its wonderful forms is one of those. The computer game industry suffers from a feedback loop no more and no less pernicious than any other in a market-driven economy, which is to say that it's very easy and low-risk to go on endlessly making games for the same market. Leaving aside for the moment the problems of continually reifying xenophobia, the overwhelming majority of those games denigrate women, deliberately or offhandedly. Quite a few people, including people of both of the major genders, have tried for quite a long time to bring about even modest change in that regard. They haven't been very successful. In large part (though not entirely) this failure is due to the character and habits of the people who actually program the games. In our research at the ACTLab my students and colleagues find that the programmers, whose population is almost exclusively young adolescent or postadolescent males, tend to live their lives in the same manner in which they write their games—with single-minded determination and a very narrow set of goals. Usually they have little in the way of social lives; they don't read books, but occasionally read comics; and they tend to perpetuate extraordinarily immature ideas of personal interaction styles. One of these is the way they relate to women. Women tend to be the same kinds of objects for them in their lives as they are in their games, and this is the heart of the problem of how pernicious the loop is: they don't believe there is a problem, because it's invisible to them. Under questioning, they intensely resist acquiring insight. They believe there is no sexism in their games, just as they believe there is no sexism in their lives.

This situation isn't surprising, really, although something in my heart keeps telling me it should be. The reality is that in the past fifteen years or so the computer game industry has gone with explosive speed from a few boys making up games for themselves and their friends to a few more boys making up games for themselves and millions of other boys. The level of sophistication hasn't changed, but the scale has changed drastically. Ethics haven't kept up, in fact have never been an issue, since the thing is market-driven and kids as a market are a relatively new phenomenon. An unanticipated product of this meaning-machine is a particular kind of monistic identity, and the contradiction here should not pass unnoticed: one of the most powerful tools for opening identity into richly textured diversity winds up being a constraining force. If this reminds us of the evolution of television from the 1950s, when programming was still experimental, on to its maturity as a medium for selling goods, it means we are paying attention.

This loops back to the question of the ludic dimension of human-computer interaction, which I've discussed at length elsewhere in other essays. Should things like computer games, which are so terrifically absorbing and which take up so much waking time—so much precious, irreplaceable waking time—be expected to possess a modicum of invention, to be able to stretch players' imaginations and skills beyond the ability to hit targets and dodge obstacles? (Not that those aren't valuable skills, but they aren't the only valuable skills either.) Should we expect play to be edifying, or on the other hand will kids manage to make anything that comes to hand edifying against all odds? Is the game market simply a dead loss from the standpoint of sexism and education, something we have to learn to live with like we had to learn to live with the Bomb? *How is it that the very young, the very talented, don't perceive the incredible power for change that has fallen to them by default—and the hideous consequences of failing to grasp that weapon when it's offered?*

As the Wellspring data took shape, I kept rereading that last sentence (which was originally part of an E-mail screed to a colleague) and marveled again and again at the shadowy reappearance of an old, old story. How very like the hero mythoid itself, I realized: how very like the ancient symbol-cluster of the Quest that underlies so many of our culture's heavily gendered, xenophobic stories of transcendence, conquest, and victory.

8

Conclusion: The Gaze of the Vampire

The illusion will be so powerful you won't be able to tell what's real and what's not.
—Steve Williams

Recently my daughter Tani said to me, "Mama, just what is it that you *do*?"

Good question.

I'm a discourse surfer. Frequently I look like a scholar. Sometimes I look like an anthropologist, sometimes a sociologist. Once in a while I'm a machine language wonk. Frequently I look like an audio engineer. And I can still tell which is the business end of a scalpel and hemostats when I have to. Of all the things I've done, discourse surfing makes me happiest. And, not unincidentally, for me in deep ways it is the most powerful tool of all the tools I've learned to use.

Discourse surfers can surf any discourse if they're good enough. I'm not that good; I have a favorite spot, at which I'm most content, but there are plenty of great coves and public places where great things happen. My favorite spot is high theory. I navigate it best by running on top. Occasionally it's wonderful, or necessary, to dive down. The depths are heady and beautiful, and if I linger too long, rapture of the deep sets in, and I begin to think I can stay down forever. Which is the signal that it's time for air.

I was thinking of all this while watching the waves with Tani. This book, the strategies deployed within it, my representational style when I address large audiences—it all sounds so light, so . . . irresponsible. I've been writing in the ironic mode for so long now that I sometimes believe the audience is taking it all seriously. I wake up thinking, "What if my tenure committee (or department head, or whatever. . .) thinks I *mean* this?"

So as this ride draws to a close, allow me a few seconds to address you directly. This may be totally unnecessary, you may have long since gotten the point, but, still . . . just in case.

Listen up. The clashing styles of this book, shifts of mood and voice, and occasional aura of irresponsibility are deliberate strategies. The subtext is that, in this brief time of upheaval and promise that always accompanies the transition between modes of experience and thought, before the long night sets in and such strategies are no longer possible, there is a window of opportunity to transform the way academic discourse in the humanities and social sciences works. In some ways this book is a sampler of possible approaches. Before breaking the rules it is necessary to understand them, so I have written, and continue to write, academic articles that are quite mainstream in character.

My goals and stakes—why I wrote the book—are brief. My daughter represents them most clearly. A slide of her appears in every talk I give, every performance I offer. In the image a two-year-old sits at an ancient 8086 clone, her tiny hands on the keyboard, a huge grin on her face. The screen radiates a brilliant yellow glow that illuminates her face and arms. Suffused with that electronic glow, her face almost seems to be taking on an illumination of its own. She seems to evince a generous permeability, an electronic porosity that is pathognomonic of the close of the mechanical age . . . and as I glance up at the image I can see the machine doing it too, as they both hover on the brink of collapsing into each other. This implosion is her moment. It is also our moment, but different from the way it belongs to her, here at the close of the mechanical age, when neurology and electronics, musculature and hydraulics, biology and technology, all hover on the edge of a stunning and irrecuperable mutual

Conclusion: The Gaze of the Vampire   167

annihilation. She will survive that implosion and emerge as what the New Testament called, in its efficient business Greek, *kaine ktisis*. New creature. We'll survive it too; we'll make it to the river, but we may not precisely cross over.

During performances, I sometimes think about the slide even when it's not on the screen. It's a mantra, that image, a way of bringing my seething thoughts back to focus. In the pressure of performance (most of my performances are improvisations on a theme, not scripted), I sometimes lose my way. When that happens, I call up the image of Tani. For me she represents not only her own future but our future. Hers, mine, and yours. The importance of this habit of mine for our purposes lies in the simple aphorism that software produces subjects. When we engage with symbolic structures of sufficient complexity, to a certain extent we synchronize our own internal symbology with those structures. In this we are carrying out our own programs as social beings. Software is merely a perspicuous example; as McLuhan pointed out seemingly so long ago, any medium serves perfectly well in this capacity. Some of you will recall that before the signing of the Nuclear Nonproliferation Treaty the Bulletin of the Atomic Scientists had a clock on the cover. For many years the clock was set very close to midnight—to Doomsday. Sometimes I think that the idea that we might destroy ourselves in a nuclear holocaust may be a better way to go than some of the other possibilities that go less remarked. The quiet death that comes when we have lost our presence in the discourses which shape our lives, when we no longer speak but are spoken—that is, when not we but our culture speaks through our mouths—is for me the most frightening. That's why for me prosthetic communication and the things it creates, specifically interactive entertainment software, the Internet, cyberspace, and virtual reality, are not a question of market share or even of content. In a fundamental McLuhanesque sense these things are parts of ourselves. As with all powerful discourses, their very existence shapes us. Since in a deep sense they are languages, it's hard to *see* what they do, because what they do is to structure seeing. They act on the systems—social, cultural, neurological—by which we make meaning. Their implicit messages change us.

My daughter reads voraciously. I see little inclination in her to suck on the glass teat in the corner of my, yes even my, living room. "Thank Ghu!" I rejoice. "My kid's not part of Jaron's postliterate generation!" Great. My backyard is safe. Then at the mall I notice the clerk is using a new type of cash register, made for people who *cannot* read. A very large electronics firm has found a growing market share. Reality could hardly be better expressed. There used to be a minigenre of science fiction devoted to stories about robots who did everything for us . . . cooked dinner, made the beds, shined our shoes. In spite of some lovely quackery, so far such devices have not happened. Instead, at the inception of the virtual age, when everything solid melts into air, we have other, far more subtle devices that don't do for us but think for us. Not computers, really—they think, in their machinic fashion, and then tell us the answers. Ubiquitous technology, which is definitive of the virtual age, is far more subtle. It doesn't tell us anything. It rearranges our thinking apparatus so that different thinking just *is*.

Soon Tani will be developing an active sexuality, and I find myself wondering which sexuality will claim her, or whether she will have the courage to choose or to improvise one for her own. And if she does, how wide a spectrum of desire will her choice be able to encompass? At her school, hard-eyed toughs from the projects cruise the perimeter of the yard, on the lookout for sex or anything else interesting; they have no doubts whatsoever about how desire works, even if they've never encountered the word. I think about theory, and watch their eyes. The phone rings, and someone asks: "Will virtual systems mean the end of gender binarism? Will virtual systems create a level playing field for everyone, regardless of ethnicity, color, gender, age, education, financial status, or the ability to load and fire semiautomatic weapons?"

And that, in fine, is why understanding how a few crazies at keyboards wind up influencing the social behavior of thousands of game players is an urgent undertaking. Is the answer, then, to outlaw violence and sexism in games? Almost certainly not. The Band-Aid approach of prohibition has lousy and ineffectual history. For example in the United States, since the Comics Code, which prohibits extreme violence in comic books, became the de facto industry standard in the late 1950s, violence among young persons has increased several *hundred* percent. If there is, in fact, some way to remold society closer to the heart's desire, it shows no visible signs of having anything to do with curing bad behavior by not looking at all those dangerous images. It's not the images, and it's not the technologies either. Neither, simply by itself, is going to "save" society. In fact, the idea that technology in and of itself is going to change the world for the better, as the myths surrounding VR would have it, is merely pernicious.

From time to time we have thought we found our Holy Grail in one or another of its manifestations . . . electricity at the turn of the century, mesmerism a bit earlier, more recently various kinds of music, drugs, and most recently perhaps, computers. The metaphor of salvation that runs as a continual shining thread throughout our traffickings with all these technologies continues unbroken into VR. So it's important to consider how we make meaning, and the battles we fight over who gets to own the meanings of our technologies. Salvation is a particularly situated cluster of meanings in Western culture. It's androcentric; it's originally Caucasian in its worldview; it's a central theme of particular national and political hegemonies. When we start talking about virtual technologies in terms of salvation we are simply retelling the old stories of technology as Holy Grail, as a hardware object, something condensed and made visible through the tellings and retellings of the cultural myths particular to us. These myths are extremely powerful, because they carry in veiled form the entire cultural force and imagined *progressus* of our Western societies. But, as the knights who searched for the Grail found out the hard way, if it's salvation that you simply must have, you will never find it in a physical object.

Thus some of our culture's most enduring storytellers tried to tell us, in their beautiful and twisted way, that the end of binary opposition is no more to be found in virtual worlds than it was to be found in computers, electricity, mesmerism, sex, drugs, or rock 'n' roll. This message is no different from what voices that are inaudible to us, because they don't speak the language of salvation, have been saying, back through time as far as we can remember—technological prosthetics are wonderful, but they aren't everything. They can change our lives, but they can't make everything okay. This merely points more directly to what or who gets to make them whatever they are, whether it's okay or not. We do that. Save sheer accident, technology has no force outside of a system of social practices. No social arrangement that we've chosen to delude ourselves is obdurate to the point of becoming a physical machine, be it a VCR or the Grail, is going to change the world for us. *We* are going to have to do it. For better or worse, with our eyes open, in the full knowledge that we ourselves are either destroying or creating our own future. No technologies, no illusions, no masks.

This book is in part an attempt to express such a sentiment and to provide some entertaining evidence for it. I've tried to give several examples of how the cultural meanings of technological prosthetics are negotiated, and of the pitfalls that lie in wait for the unwary. A case in point is the complex interaction between Sarah, the Oshkosh woman with multiple personalities, and a legal system that attempted to grope with the traffic between conventional ideas of person and the reality of the person(s) before them. The questions raised there, which Judge Hawley remarked were about splitting some very fine hairs, were serious attempts to open space for new interpretations of what counts as a person in a world in which fragmentation and multiplicity occasionally push themselves into public awareness in fairly undeniable ways.

Indirectly, the Oshkosh event points out the troubled locus of conflicting forces that marks out the space of the individual in modern society. How these forces merge and separate, and the battles between them, are perspicuous engagements in the war of desire and technology—the complex emergence not of new social but new personal formations, arising from the contested zone at the boundaries between the machinic assemblages of commodification, simulation, political power, and the inexpungible human desire for sociality and love.

Julie, the cross-dressing psychiatrist, demonstrated simultaneously the therapeutic possibilities of the virtual mode and the complex and difficult ways in which on-line participants choose to ground themselves in the expectation of a "true identity" against which other quasi-identities may be judged. In this they evinced what may have been the last manifestation of such a sensibility in the virtual world. Participants who believed themselves to be unquestionably rooted in specific identities, which were grounded in biological "facts" and reinforced by mutual affirmations in face-to-face social interactions, were poorly prepared to quickly relinquish those expectations in the virtual world. In this circumstance we can also get a taste of how pain can work to enforce the boundaries between real and virtual, and also to see—in the case of the physically challenged women who could not find sufficient resonance between Julie's professed off-line life and their own—an ineluctable separation between real and virtual modes. Thus, as the boundaries between worlds become increasingly porous, it appears that not quite all that is solid may be permitted to melt into air. There are now and in all probability will continue to be places, both virtual and physical in character, in which the lessons of the virtual communities will have questionable effect because of their capacity to produce too much cognitive dissonance with traditional customs and older received knowledges.

Recalling the profound sense of violation felt by some of the women in the Joan incident, let's look at one final example of violation and virtuality. Recently the inhabitants of LambdaMOO, the first experimental MOO community, experienced their first taste of what the press was quick to call "rape." In this event—heralded with the same shocked and bewildered response as was Joan Green's unmasking almost ten years previous—a "woman" (a presumably biologically female person who performed woman as her social role) was virtually molested by another inhabitant of the virtual environment who identified himself as "male." A surprising aspect of the LambdaMOO event was how the term *rape* itself was adopted relatively unproblematically by many of the participants in the debate. Thus the metaphoric character of the act became its chief defining characteristic, and this is a double-edged weapon that carries with it its own difficulties. The problematic term was not adopted easily by everyone. Amy Bruckman, founder of MIT's MediaMOO and a formidable researcher, was among the first to problematize it, along with Pavel Curtis, founder of LambdaMOO and originator of the code upon which most MOOs are based. Both researchers felt that *rape* should be a privileged term, referring to physical violation in physically grounded circumstances—that is, when no logging out is possible. Otherwise, the term becomes so broad as to be useless to express outrage at more hurtful things. I heartily agree with this view. I don't think that the concept of violation is sufficiently coextensive with the concept of rape that the two terms can collapse, but apparently the term has such social resonance that it persists in spite of efforts on the part of many of the participants to dislodge it and replace it with one more suited to the virtual mode.

The lesson here is that the term *rape* as it was employed in Oshkosh carries a distinctly different constellation of codings than the term used in the debates surrounding the LambdaMOO event. Moreover, what happened in Oshkosh varies in its ascribed meaning depending upon whose interests are foregrounded. The state of Wisconsin had specific interests in bringing a violator to justice, even though his victim (Franny or Sarah?) did not believe that a rape had occurred. The issue revolved around particular definitions of competence, and because under Wisconsin law multiple personality is de facto mental disease, these tended to obscure the issue of whether Franny was a competent individual in her own right and thus capable of participating in a consenting sexual act.

The term *multiplicity* also appears in both accounts, and again it is multivalent. The multiple subjectivity experienced by the physical person one of whose on-line personae is a rapist in LambdaMOO is not the same multiple subjectivity experienced by Sarah (or for that matter, Franny) in a park in Oshkosh with the man who assaulted her.

It is possible, on occasion, to reveal and trace the ramification of power structures which, concomitant to their establishment, act to constrain rather than foster diversity. For example, Marie Louise Roberts (1994) traces the attempt on the part of early French feminists to reconstruct or eliminate altogether the structures of gender inequality. In her work *Civilization Without Sexes,* she finds in the last analysis that the attempt failed because gender inequality was a societal way to stabilize the flow of property and hence power in a propertied state through the male line. Of course, this social device has its counterpart in various forms in other cultures. In this book my search is for something different: to reveal and trace the ramification of power structures which, concomitant to their establishment, act to constrain rather than enhance the strong human drive—recently emergent—to rewrite the social and cultural form, in its manifestation as the visible body, that we are constrained to take. This is not the same thing as discussing how to create free men and women, or even free citizens, because what I am suggesting is that we call into question the structure of meaning production by which we recognize each other as human. From a standpoint of theory, this is a gnarly enterprise. One of the problems with academic discourse is that by its nature there is a place where theory as we now understand it falls short of being an adequate modeling or predictive tool. As Audre Lorde pointed out, theory is one of the master's tools. The structures by which the world is apprehended are inaccessible to change by theory, which, by its nature, is descriptive and predictive and can make some phenomena visible that have previously been obscure, but is not the best choice for making interventions. The structures of interest here are deeper and more fugitive by nature than that. They may be, as my current studies of and experiments with performance seem to show, vulnerable to a different set of tools.

With regard to virtual systems, certain conditions must be met before new kinds of tools can be found. One is management of the substrate around which virtual social formations are constituted. With text-based communities, the substrate is the program code: Will it be predictable in its responses, but still flexible and pliable to changing needs and purposes; or failing that, how resistant to disruption can it be made? In the case of CommuniTree we saw a complex community in the early stages of formation, a loose aggregation of technophiles with a spiritual and intellectual predilection who met in cyberspace for the first time. It is significant that after a time in cyberspace many of these early personauts were overcome by the need to engage other sensibilities besides the textual, and formed a face-to-face discussion group that met weekly thereafter. Not without significance, this unconscious strategy prolonged the group's longevity far beyond the sacking and destruction of the Tree itself. The program code underwent a partial translation from the machine to a (biological) human assemblage: a proper cyborg move. The young programmers who had come to the Tree for other purposes learned the first hard cyberspace lessons from their experience, and went on to attempt in various ways to bulletproof their own trees—generally with great success. More than ten years later, some of those early cyber-horticultural experiments continue to thrive, updated again and again to meet new challenges and opportunities. In their continuing evolution perhaps we are witnessing practical examples of cyborg speciation, the evolution of complex assemblages of humans and technological prostheses driven by a mutual need for survival.

Another condition is dissemination of information across groups with divergent epistemes and aesthetics. In this book one example is innovation at the Atari Lab. Once the time of the individual hacker as source of all creativity had passed, important pieces of the puzzle of enabling technology had to arise in corporate milieux. The golden window at Atari was a perspicuous instance of how the implications of new technologies are (or are not) negotiated across the boundaries of corporate management and basic technological inquiry. One of the primary lessons from the demise of the Atari Lab is in the way the meaning of terms such as *research* did not translate across the boundaries of competing social groups. This should have been clear from the Arthur group's experiences with early forms of E-mail, which existed in the lab and in other departments at Atari, but apparently no alarm was sounded. The same situation is ubiquitous in the nets. Because cyberspace is vast, the multivalent quality of common terms easily escapes notice, even though cybernauts had to learn quite early that even the simplest expressions do not pass from one keyboard to another without difficulties in translation. The development of emoticons—shorthand ways of attaching specific emotions to particular utterances—was a direct consequence of ferocious misunderstandings over simple textual utterances far back at the dawn of the very first networks.

Another lesson from the abrupt end of the lab was how competing groups understood (or failed to understand) the long-range, rather than short-term, implications of prosthetic communication. Differences in understanding were caused in part by differences in age and class, in goal horizons, and in particular in the appropriation of powerful technosocial tools for aggrandizement in terms of market share. In this sense the Atari Lab was a useful (if painful) test bed, in which several of the social worlds that are competing to own culturally loaded terms such as *research* played out some of the possible conflicts. The size of the experiential and philosophical gulf that separated them makes their experience useful in virtual systems research, since its high visibility presents an entry point into studies of more subtle articulations of difference within high-technology workplaces. Inevitably it foregrounds the problems that arise when established power structures attempt to colonize new discourses during their emergent and organizational phases. (Bruno Latour means something similar when he refers to the time before the "black box" is closed.)

In the course of the Atari story I used the clumsy term *technoepistemology,* by which I attempted to foreground the way technologies are treated (here by me and elsewhere by others) either as social productions or as the physical residue of contestations over the distribution of capital and other resources. In cyborg studies and more traditional arenas (as, e.g., in the so-called Strong Programme in the sociology of innovation), technologies are visible and frequently material evidence of struggles over meaning. They don't exist outside of complex belief systems in whose social and political frames they are embedded. Their apparent obduracy is an artifact, a technology of its own. A VCR remote control is merely a ritual object in the absence of the dense social networks, capital structures, and manufacturer-driven expectations that manifest as cable and satellite technology, market share, leisure time, and entertainment.

In my small corner of the academic vineyard, from time to time my sympathies are with those who study how the peculiar cultural object we have named technology is constructed and how its complex meanings are negotiated among the many factions who seek to control them. This struggle is related in certain ways to the earlier struggle to control the meaning of the term *progress* in the late nineteenth century. In this book about war and desire of a different kind I have taken a number of instances in which various kinds of technologies have solidified, and shown something of the gritty circumstances surrounding their solidification. In doing so I have chosen some methods of cultural representation that by usual academic standards are, perhaps, unconventional. As I may or may not have mentioned already, this is a deliberate and considered strategy. At the heart of my effort is the growing belief that the space of interaction between the academic and other worlds and between academic worlds themselves is undergoing deep and disturbing change, in complex cause-effect interaction with the emergence of new communication prosthetics. The burgeoning Internet holds the chimeric promise of paperless essays, as well as the frightening prospect of bodiless conventions— frightening because we academics tend to be a cloistered species anyway, and we have learned that the social institution of the convention is an easily negotiated respite that is not well served by the virtual mode. But more urgently and quite apart from whatever changes technological prosthetics may bring to the academy, I sense in the wind that the hoary and infinitely serviceable methods of representation that have worked so well for so long are beginning to break down, and that some academics are beginning to search—perhaps almost unconsciously—for new ways to convey their work to their peers.

With this thought firmly in mind, it may be clearer that the style of this book—and, for those who have met either of my two major personae at conferences, the style of personal presentation that it underscores—is a deliberate and considered intervention. In its seemingly haphazard and rambling style is embedded a careful and occasionally grim strategy. The purpose of this move is to open new possibilities for exchanging information at the professional level. As with any move toward change, it is greeted with deep suspicion in some circles and with guarded hope in others. Its unabashed gesture of performance, both in person and on the page, is seen as inappropriate in some quarters and as useful in its way in others. I don't expect the gesture of performance to be embraced with unqualified abandon or with anything approaching uniformity. But I do suggest that the new formations of academic thought that emerge at the interface between scholarly reportage and the performative gesture hold significant and promising power for rethinking what a university is and ought to be, here at the close of the mechanical age—mechanical age in all its meanings, including the broader sense of intellectual and logical assemblage. We no longer live in a world in which information conserves itself primarily in textual objects called books. In a world in which not only information but also meaning struggles to escape its customary channels, perhaps the best way to serve the scholarly muse may not be to continue to play out the moves that served perfectly in the age of the scriptorium and the inescapable facticity of data. Of course there was nothing natural or essential about the scriptorium or about monkish pursuits either. They, too, emerged from the inescapable needs of their age, of a time when, to detourn Stewart Brand, information needed not to be free but to conserve itself and its power with a view to better times ahead. Now that we live, tentatively but inescapably, at the threshold of a new and unsettling age, perhaps it's time to reimagine the scholarly enterprise in terms of this new age—terms under which academics in the humanities and social sciences cannot be the conservators of stable knowledges that are crystallized in books and belief systems, but rather in which the critical importance to human growth and fulfillment that the humanities and social sciences provide within the university structure can drive the institution of higher education to reemerge in a form that can carry it beyond the so-called information revolution, without compromising its mission as conservator of the best of whatever this brawling, struggling thing we call humanity is or may yet come to be.

And so we come by this circuitous route to the Vampire Lestat, the novelist Anne Rice's antihero of the Vampire Chronicles. The vampire has always been a problematic figure in literature, capitalized upon for its implications of contamination, subjection, violation, and, more recently, uncontrolled exchange of body fluids. Recently we've seen another revival of interest in the vampire, expressed in pop culture by such plays and films as *Dracula, Bram Stoker's Dracula, The Wild Ones, The Hunger, Transylvania 6-5000,* and so on. Maybe we are already into nostalgia mode, longing for a time when transgressing the body's physical envelope might lead to an eroticized subjection, but not as surely to death as vampirism in the age of AIDS.

Lestat is a liminal creature and—though not to belabor the obvious—a cyborg. Cyborgs are boundary creatures, not only human/machine but creatures of cultural interstice as well; and Lestat inhabits the boundaries between death and life, temporality and eternity, French and English, gay and straight, man and woman, good and evil. He nicely exemplifies a style of cyborg existence, capturing the pain and complexity of attempting to adapt to a society, a lifestyle, a language, a culture, an epistemology, even in Lestat's case a species, that is not one's own. Lestat is a vampire for our seasons, struggling with the swiftly changing meanings of what it is to be human or, for that matter, unhuman.

Since I started researching and writing this book I've been conducting a thought experiment with Lestat—sending him back to the university, to encounter and learn to cope with the modern academic milieu.
Once there, he seemed to take on a life of his own. He studied cyborg
theory and cultural theory, and he earned a Ph.D. in anthropology.

Lestat grapples continually with his vampire nature, trying to
thrash out workable ethics in all the different worlds he inhabits, each
of which he inhabits only partially. Lestat is fascinated by humans,
whom he prefers to call mortals—that is, beings who are able to die.
He is fascinated, first, because he is powerfully drawn to human
blood, and for him human blood evokes deep, complex sensual experiences. He can smell and hear the rich, fragrant blood whispering
and thundering through the bodies of his mortal friends, the hot thick
blood that circumscribes and defines mortality for him. And, second,
it is mortality which holds endless fascination for Lestat, who stands
partly outside human life and is simultaneously deeply meshed within
it; for his mortal friends will inevitably age and eventually perish;
while, barring accident, he will continue through time, forever tasting
but never fully locked into the world of sensual experience and sensory adventure.

This is the poignancy of the gaze of the vampire. The naive, preuni-
versity Lestat saw humans transfixed by the arrow of time, caught
up in the tragedy and glory of living in history, inhabiting a temporal
narrative produced and supported by dense social networks of beliefs
and practices from which he himself was excluded. Around that fact
revolved much of Lestat's philosophy.

In all this I have been describing the Vampire Lestat familiar from
Rice's Vampire Chronicles, but the Anthropologist Lestat is a new
creature who perceives things somewhat differently. He has acquired
a new kind of vision, still vampiric, but now modulated by the experience of being immersed in cultural theory. He also has a vocabulary
for things that he previously could not articulate. With this new vocabulary of vision the Anthropologist Lestat's vampire gaze sees humans transfixed not only by the arrow of time but in addition by the

sword of *subject position*—mortals locked in place by the construction and maintenance of a speaking-being-in-time from which, by virtue of his position outside human consciousness, Lestat himself is also excluded.

There is a poignancy to this exclusion and the consequent longings it engenders. With his vampire gaze, Lestat sees subjectivity as possibility, and thus the myriad aspects of subjectivity that mortals take for granted as no more than boats temporarily at anchor in a sea of possibilities. But here the crosscurrents of fiction and physicality, desire and technology, eddy and conflict. The social sea of possibility is rife with dangerous shoals, and not all subject positions have the same implications and consequences. The masquerade of gender is symptomatic but not definitive. Those who live their lives by masquerade of whatever kind—those who must pass in order to live, whether passing means ethnicity or color or nationality or gender, skill level or professional accomplishment—know and understand this fact quite well.

I've mentioned that I have huge stakes in these arguments, and that the anthropologist Lestat is not simply a rhetorical device. As a transgendered academic who lives by choice in the boundaries between subject positions, I share a portion of Lestat's vampire gaze. And of course the vampiric way of seeing is shared by others who are themselves directly engaged in the wonder and terror of masquerade. Since Glória Anzaldúa created room in academic discourses in which to write the border body, which inhabits the space she calls the "thin edge of barbwire," there are those who live in other boundaries who are fortunate enough to have also benefited from her work. Standing in the hard brilliance of Anzaldúa's words, I am engaged, with many other theorists, performers, and artists, in making a clear space within discourses of gender and performance for transgender theory. In cyberspace the transgendered body is the natural body. The nets are spaces of transformation, identity factories in which bodies are meaning machines, and transgender—identity as performance, as play, as wrench in the smooth gears of the social apparatus of vision—is the ground state. This sounds like a truism now, but think back to the time, not so long ago, when Joan Green caused such trauma with no more than fingers on a keyboard.

Conversely—and, I think, obviously—in physical space the transgendered body is the unnatural body. Unnatural recalls monstrous, in its alternative meaning as the French *montrer*, showing forth, making visible. The transgendered body is a screen, upon which is projected the war between unnatural and natural, speech and silence, monstration and effacement. The natural body is invisible, in the sense that as a cultural production it is unproblematic in its just-thereness. In physical space the natural body is one whose performance is invisible, and by that invisibility the illusory refractoriness of the materialized discursivity that is the social subject under the law is maintained. It is the physicality, simultaneously lived and imagined, which expresses the default subject position in the virtual age, and which by its enunciation calls into question not simply the masquerade of gender but the facticity of social identity *tout court*.

But all is not play in the virtual worlds. In observing social interaction in cyberspace we find that while some aspects of meaning production escape traditional cultural coding, many things in the nets are in fact naturalized; and this more subtle naturalization can easily pass unnoticed. For example, entry to the world of virtual community requires high levels of skills in the English language and a high level of technical proficiency, but this annoying fact usually passes unremarked. Many researchers, some quite naively, tend to see cyberspace as a space of possibility precisely because it can give the (facile) illusion of a level playing field. Of course to believe that in cyberspace everyone is equal merely because the codings that have attached themselves to voice quality and physical appearance have been uncoupled from their referents, and that this uncoupling provides a sensation that might be perceived as inherently liberatory, is to misunderstand how power works.

Which brings us finally to the Dark Gift.

Lestat the Vampire has the power to confer the Dark Gift—to

make new vampires. These new vampires then also acquire the dangerous knowledge of the partiality of the mortal gaze. But although vampires' senses are extremely acute, they are not omniscient; their awareness of the limits of human vision and the vision that is possible even without the Dark Gift flow from their cyborg nature, simultaneously part of and separate, inside and outside, inhabiting Anzaldùa's thin edge of barbwire which painfully announces the dangerous outer limits of experientiality between cultures, economies, and subjectivities. They invoke by their simple existence the disruption of classificatory schemata that calls traditional identity formation into question.

The Anthropologist Lestat realizes that as an anthropologist vampire he has the power to confer a new and different Dark Gift. And here, of course, the metaphor shades into the actual, and the work begins. The new Dark Gift is the passing on of the newly transformed vampire gaze, the visual knowledge which makes the machineries of subjectivity visible and the nuts and bolts that hold the surface of reality together stand out from the background. But for us, living in the boundaries between the dying world of safely grounded epistemologies and the querulously emergent world of cyborg instrumentalities, we face the problem of the real, and not the metaphorical Dark Gift. Because if such vampires, vampires of subjectivity, really do exist, then none of us is safe—safe, that is, within our traditionally bounded subject positions, our accustomed places in a rapidly shifting world. We are no longer unproblematically secure within the nest of our location technologies, whose function for us (as opposed to for our political apparatus) is to constantly reassure us that we are without question ourselves, singular, bounded, conscious, rational; the end product of hundreds of years of societal evolution in complex dialogue with technology as Other and with gender as an othering machine. The vampire of subjectivity sees the play of identity from the metalevel, sees the fragrant possibilities of multiple voice and subject position, the endless refraction of desire, with a visual apparatus that has become irreducibly and fatally different. Once one receives this Dark Gift, there is no way back to a simpler and less problematic time. The gaze of the vampire, once achieved, cannot be repudiated; it changes vision forever.

As we stand together at the close of the mechanical age, in the ruins of a system of visual knowledge whose cultural purpose was to ground and authorize sovereign subjectivity, that such vampires *do* exist is for me the challenge and the promise of virtual systems. The war of desire and technology is a war of transformation, in which, if we look deeply enough, we can make out the lineaments of our own vampire future. Ultimately the gaze of the vampire is our own transfigured and transfiguring vision. Claiming that vision is our task and our celebration.

I look forward eagerly to continuing this high adventure with you—uttering the vision and claiming it—the adventure that is our future, as we immerse ourselves ever more deeply in our own technologies; as the boundaries between our technologies and ourselves continue to implode; as we inexorably become creatures that we cannot even now imagine. It is a moment which simultaneously holds immense threat and immense promise. I don't want to lose sight of either, because we need to guide ourselves—remember *cyber* means steer—in all our assembled forms and multiple selves right between the two towers of promise and danger, of desire and technology. In the space between them lies the path to our adventure at the dawn of the virtual age, the adventure which belongs to our time and which is ours alone.

Well met in cyberspace.

Notes

Sources for the Epigraphs

The three epigraphs to this book are, in order, from James Clifford's essay "Identity in Mashpee," in James Clifford, *The Predicament of Culture* (Cambridge, MA: Harvard University Press, 1988); Anselm Strauss's introduction to Strauss (ed.), *G. H. Mead on Social Psychology* (Chicago: University of Chicago Press, 1978); and Donna Haraway's postscript to "Cyborgs at Large: An Interview with Donna Haraway," in Constance Penley and Andrew Ross (eds.), *Technoculture* (Minneapolis: University of Minnesota Press, 1991).

Introduction: Sex, Death, and Machinery, or How I Fell in Love with My Prosthesis

1. This is the first instance of the collapse of fiction and fact (whatever that is), narratization and description, that the style of this essay implies. Being a novelist at heart causes me to create krasis narratives, and it's hard to know to what depth I need to explicate them. Consequently let's try treating these two descriptive paragraphs as exemplary, to an extent that I will not carry on into the rest of the text. Both events are emblematic rather than specific. The bedroom is a combination of bedrooms from at least four different locales, including the young Kal-el's room on the farm in *Superman I*. There was no friend present; for reasons of my own I wanted to decenter the moment of discovery. Peering over a 24 24 console would have been impossible in 1955, since the state of the art was three-track recording, and at any rate I was too tall to have my nose at that level; the scene combines visits to various control rooms beginning in the late 1940s and extending into the 1970s, and when I was a preteen to pilgrimages to the transmitter of WOR itself, which, with its black bakelite monoliths and glowing

1920-style power meters, resembled most closely some science-fiction author's depiction of mighty forces coiled to spring. There was little doubt in my mind that much of the early cinematic depictions of technology as mysterious and inexplicable power, as exemplified in *Metropolis*, came from the movie set designers' own visits to the few instantiations of technology at work that yet existed—i.e., the control rooms of the few radio stations that maintained remote transmitter sites. These were invariably located far from populated areas, usually in swamps, thus specifically invoking the motif of lonely isolation in spooky circumstances.

2. All of this, of course, is about the interplay between communication technology, prosthetic community, the human body, and the uses of pleasure.

3. For some reason this sort of thing—having someone barge into my humdrum life and drag me off on some adventure—keeps happening, and I have gotten more good story material in such fashion than I like to admit.

4. This is perhaps the most egregious point of convergence of the two theses I have been pursuing. A more detailed description and analysis of the oddly interdependent issues of lesbian separatism and transgender can be found in my "other" book, *The Gaze of the Vampire: Tales from the Edges of Identity*.

5. My use of the word *talk* to refer to writing and reading is both playful and a considered position. Part of the work of this essay is to play in the boundaries between speech and writing as I discuss the play I observe in electronically prostheticized human interaction. A typical example is a letter waiting in my E-mail box that begins, "Good to read from you."

6. Lippman had been developing these ideas in discussions at the MIT Media Lab over a period of time beginning in the early 1980s, but they were perhaps best captured by Stuart Brand in his recounting of talks with Lippman in *The Media Lab: Inventing the Future at MIT* (1987).

7. The invention of *SpaceWar* is variously dated. Laurel (1991) puts it at 1962.

8. In particular I am referring to Deleuze and Guattari's discussions of deterritorialization and multiplicity in *Anti-Oedipus* (1983) and *A Thousand Plateaus* (1987), Virilio in *The Aesthetics of Disappearance* (1991a) and *The Light of Speed* (1991b), and Manuel De Landa in *War in the Age of Intelligent Machines* (1991), annotated fully in the bibliography.

9. I refer to Barker as "she" here without really being sure what s/he is. Some colleagues have assured me that Barker is a woman. Others claim that because of the spelling of the first name, Barker must be a man. Certainly this is something that should have been cleared up before publication, but I rather enjoy the confusion and the debates thus precipitated.

10. At the time I was first thrashing this out I had recently read Bruno Latour's *The Pasteurization of France* (1988) in its French incarnation, *Les Microbes: Guerre et paix suivi les irreductions.* As I struggled to regain whatever fluency in French I may have previously possessed, I completely missed Latour's pun on Tolstoy in the title of the book. It must have stuck around in the background.

11. Few of these adjectives, like *bloodthirsty* and *infamous,* are accidental, and I am fully aware of their tendentious character. These stories are experimental, and part of the experiment is to see how much (if any) of what I might term "dangerous" story forms can be recuperated into a different discourse without contaminating it (another deliberate word choice). The events at the Atari Lab are emblematic of what happened when the first generation of graduates—bright, dedicated, and to an extent thrillingly conscious of the liberatory potential of their creations—hit the buzz saw of commodification and then the street.

12. There are wide variations in the estimates of Habitat's actual population, even within Fujitsu. The actual figure is probably lower, but how much lower is uncertain.

13. Morningstar and Farmer maintain that it never occurred to them that the characters might want to have sex; they were too preoccupied with just getting characters to look reasonably right and to be able to walk around. It is also possible that LucasFilm might have frowned on the idea, had it arisen at the time. It is not clear whether Fujitsu would have exercised the same scruples, nor that it would have made much difference vis-à-vis sexual activity within the simulation.

14. My use of the term *computer-based* is already becoming an anachronism, because the meanings of culturally defined objects such as television, telephone, cable, and computers, and the boundaries between them, are already in hot debate and increasing flux. Nicholas Negroponte had already pointed out in the late 1970s that there would soon come a time when there might be more MIPS (a measurement of processor speed) in kitchen appliances than in the objects commonly called computers. This development prefigures, in part at least, the cultural redefinition, now under way, of these objects. It is partly driven by economics and partly by the effect of ubiquitous technology (technology so familiar as to be culturally invisible) on engineers' interpretations of the boundaries of their specialties, as well as ubiquitous technology's effect on the cultural paradigm of biological-machinic binarism. An exhilarating and problematic time.

15. In *Tales of Neveryon* (Delany 1979).

16. I want to emphasize that this sort of thing, i.e., quoting from nonexistent

188 Notes to Chapter 1

work, is meant in a wholly humorous way. However, the case in point had its beginnings in a real and somewhat bizarre event. When I first came to the History of Consciousness program at the University of California at Santa Cruz, I had several dreams in which I was reading scholarly papers written by Haraway. Later, while writing a critique of some aspect of scientific research I absentmindedly quoted from one of the papers I'd dreamed about, confusing it in my fevered brain with a "real" Haraway paper. Some time later, while trying to attribute page and line, I realized that the paper I'd cited was in physical terms nonexistent. The quote itself, however, whatever its true source in my memory, was exactly apt and productively useful. I mentioned this to Haraway, who jokingly requested coauthorship if I ever wrote out the papers I'd dreamed I read. In retrospect this was a rather novel instantiation of the mentoring relationship, neatly avoiding problems of age and experience, while evincing several of the advantages of virtuality as well as a considerable amount of tribality. Virtual mentoring, or shamanistic training? In regard to the quote, Haraway actually said, "Refuse closure and insist upon situation"; I have interpolated "Seek multiplicity."

17. I left this sentence in because it's fun. When I first wrote it, I had a lot of convincing to do, and a lot of forums to legitimize. Now academic panels on "virtual community" pop up like mushrooms, but times have changed so fast that the sentence makes me chuckle.

Chapter 1. Collective Structures

1. Orishas and loas are the gods of Haitian and certain Afro-Caribbean religious traditions such as Voudoun or "voodoo." Toward the end of *Count Zero* the protagonists discover that certain emergent phenomena in the Net—sentient beings which are unwarrantable to human or machine agency—are in fact loas. This raises the question of whether the loas invaded the Net, or originated there, or manifested as a consequence of distributed human expectation.

2. Insofar as "real" people approach the condition of bodilessness, they do indeed still make love, as quite distinct from having sex. For a fictionalized but quite accurate account, cf. Varley (1986).

3. Rabinow (1991).

4. The term *materialized discursivity* is from the work of Donna Haraway.

5. Butler in *Gender Trouble* (1990), Mercer in "Black Hairstyle Politics," from *New Formations* 3 (1987).

6. In discussing Foucault's work, Michel de Certeau points out that the moves that transform the physical citizen into what I called a little discourse are themselves nondiscursive, but that these nondiscursive moves, which are "privileged for social and historical reasons that remain to be explained," are at the heart of the structure of contemporary scientific knowledge. A wonderfully leading remark.

7. Thus in this sense Truddi is a true actant, in that she exists primarily as a (re)collection of functions in the Truddi narrative.

8. Goodeve (1989, 120).

Chapter 2. *Risking Themselves:* Identity in Oshkosh

1. Once we have done our cutaway to Oshkosh, the methodology and textual style become more resolutely experimental than before, if that's possible. Consequently more than a few words of explanation follow here. The style of the piece is intended to evoke multiplicity, first by jump-cutting between the (problematic) firsthand viewpoint of the trial itself and the theoretical discussions of medicopsychological texts that interrupt the account of the trial and each other. In addition, neither of the two main threads, taken separately, is meant to be read as a linear narrative. I have taken portions of Colin Ross's text out of the order in which he presents them in the primary source. In this action I am using Ross's theory to construct a different sort of theoretical ambiance than Ross himself might like. It is an act of wholesale appropriation in a spirit of experimentation, and I do not guarantee the results. My account of the trial itself should also be treated with suspicion. Although the viewpoint shifts into and out of first person, I was not present at the trial, nor were the courtroom scenes taken from official court transcripts, which were prohibitively expensive. To this extent the piece is meant to invoke "Identity in Mashpee" but not to duplicate it. It is in no sense a traditionally anthropological account. My intent is rather to experiment with an alternative quasi-anthropological storytelling, accompanied by fair warning that we are outside the bounds of traditional anthropological description. All courtroom scenes are reconstructions created through interviews with persons who were themselves present, and occasionally with the aid of transcriptions from tape recordings of portions of the testimony. In this regard I have relied heavily upon conversations with Cynthia Gorney, who was present at the trial as a reporter for the *Washington Post*, and upon material provided by Deborah Bradley, Mark Hargrove, and Louise Johnson. Data gathering was of the type generally characterized as "in depth," because I was interested, in an as-yet-unwritten longer account, in creating an atmospheric piece that conveyed my own sense of the trial and

its implications. The dialogue within quotes comes from my interviews with persons who were present or who had professional or nonprofessional contacts with any of the principals, and where my notes fail, from Gorney's verbatim transcriptions. But even where dialogue is quoted, there is no guarantee that things are in any sense pristine. On occasion I have added dialogue from other parts of the transcriptions, deleted portions of the testimony, collapsed several persons into one, changed some names and not others, and in general constructed a fictional narrative which hews rather closely to that of the trial itself but which is not identical to it. Where I describe gestures, these come from descriptions of gestures made by the participants and reported by my informants. In the case of atmospheric phrases (e.g., media vans, the sound of air conditioning, something metallic dropping in the hallway), I elicited such as were available and in most cases did not cross-check them among informants. For me, the problems of producing the Oshkosh narrative are the obverse of the problems I faced when writing my forthcoming science fiction novel *Ktahmet*, which is heavily based on material that I simply copied verbatim from my diaries. In writing *Ktahmet* the problem was the real-life character of the fictional narrative (Betsy Wollheim, my editor, was fond of yelling, "Even if it's true, it's fiction"), while in writing "Identity in Oshkosh" the problem was the fictional character of the real-life narrative.

2. In "The *Empire* Strikes Back: A Posttranssexual Manifesto," in Epstein and Straub (eds.), *Body Guards: The Cultural Politics of Gender Ambiguity* (1991).

3. In Foucault, "The Spectacle of the Scaffold," from *Discipline and Punish* (1977).

Chapter 3. *In Novel Conditions:* The Cross-Dressing Psychiatrist

1. The methodology of this section is diverse. First, there is a great deal of what has been called the new thick description, namely, archives of on-line conversation. This is made possible by the technological character of text-based virtual communities. In most modem programs anything that passes across the screen can be written to a file. The floppy disk has become the cyberanthropologist's field notebook; in virtual social environments nothing escapes its panoptic gaze. Thus there are simple means of preserving the entire conversational records of text-based virtual communities. In the instance of graphic-based virtual communities, this is still possible, but not for every participant and not without some hacking. In the case of the chapter on CommuniTree, I had complete archives of the Tree community back to its inception, but then discovered that material that was more pertinent to my

description was not part of the archive because it had not taken place on-line. In the case of "The Cross-Dressing Psychiatrist" I first heard of Julie (whose prototype, Joan Green, has been described by Lindsy Van Gelder, *vide infra*) from acquaintances who were participants in the chat lines. Then, through an odd series of circumstances, when the Julie persona began to unravel I discovered that in an earlier context I had already met the psychiatrist involved.

My account of Lewin's creation of the Julie persona is a pastiche. Very little of it comes from transcriptions. Most is from interviews with participants in chat environments in which notable deceptions occurred. At first the stories that involved reporting conversations with or about Julie were fragmentary and even contradictory; for a while Julie came across as an older woman rather than a young one, and that was how I reported her in my first write-ups. At least one informant said that Julie could only type with a headstick, a device used by people who do not have the use of their hands, and I wrote that up too, thus giving Julie more of a complex persona than any of us had intended. At the time it seemed not unreasonable that a physically challenged person might participate in chat this way, but in fact few "normally" abled chatline habitués would have the patience to wait for a headstick typist; in the 1990s chatlines tend to be torrents of simultaneous high-speed typing.

An earlier insightful account of the incident upon which the Julie events are based was published by Lindsy Van Gelder as "The Strange Case of the Electronic Woman," first in *Ms.* Magazine (1985) and later in Rob Kling's anthology *Computerization and Controversy: Value Conflicts and Social Choices* (Boston 1991). I have used her thorough and emotionally lively account to inform mine, and have paraphrased her work in two instances, one in regard to Julie's allying herself with the police during her convalescence (which made no sense as recorded in my notes), and the other in her depiction of the psychiatrist as using his Joan persona "to do good," which was not in my notes at all and which I found alternately hilarious and sad, and which, I felt, added a remarkable dimension to Lewin's actions. When I first wrote up my version of the incident I pseudonymized the psychiatrist as I do here, and although Van Gelder used his "real" (legal) name, I have retained the pseudonym in this version because my account collapses several people from different chat systems who engaged in similar acts. I doubt that this will cause any confusion, but in case it does, be advised that we are discussing essentially the same events. Van Gelder published first in both instances.

In regard to the opening section on the relationship between the SCA, programming, and California neopaganism, in response to a query by Carolyn Clark I find nothing causal about this provocative juxtaposition and

did not intend to imply one—not here, at any rate—except to note that two
of the most important individuals in contemporary neopaganism were active
in northern California during this period. One is Starhawk, the author of
The Spiral Dance, and the other, who preferred anonymity, founded what
is arguably the largest neopagan networking organization and is a programmer and systems consultant. For better or worse, however, my research has
consistently demonstrated an overwhelming juxtaposition of interests between northern California programmers and neopagans, and when one adds
in the extremely peculiar incident with the physicists and the metaphase
typewriter (*vide infra*), one is left with an inescapable feeling that something
causal is happening.

With regard to Role Playing Games (RPGs), I collected my data as a participant observer in several RPG communities in northern and southern California, beginning in 1979 in Bonny Doon with the kind assistance of Preston
Q. Boomer, a mathematics instructor and RPG master at San Lorenzo High
School, and continuing through 1989 with D&D groups in the Santa Clara
Valley, Scotts Valley, and San Diego. Boomer played D&D on the grand
scale, involving major Silicon Valley corporations fielding strike teams for
full-scale field maneuvers (for example, a scuba team from IBM once staged
a surprise assault on Boomer's swimming pool to cut off the water supply
to his watercannon), and his story alone should occupy at least a chapter
in this book. I attended the SCA tournaments of which I write here, in 1983
in Oakland and throughout the late 1980s in northern and southern California, in full regalia as Ülfedínn öd Vagfÿaråndi, an Elder (female) Mage, and
subsequently waded through all four removals (a Middle Ages term meaning
sixteen courses) of the banquets. My on-line D&D data gathering began in
1980 at 300 baud with the original Mines of Moria. At that time inexpensive
modems did not exist, and my little modem consisted of a data latch and
decoder chip in hardware and a machine language program (the first 6502
machine language program I wrote) to drive it.

The research underlying the stories of MUDs, MOOs, MUSEs, MUSHes,
MUCKs and other multiple-user social environments recounted herein is entirely my own, both from participant observation and on- and off-line interviews. I am not terribly fond of most D&D, so the data gathering was not,
as some have alleged, continuous unalloyed pleasure. This task was made
easier by ACTLab.rtf.utexas.edu, the Advanced Communication Technologies Laboratory M** host machine, and especially by John Garnett, who
graciously consented to supervise the four MUDs and two MOOs that originally ran on the ACTLab system; by Allan Alford, a.k.a. chiphead, who
masterminded PointMOOTt, actlab's best worked-out and most ill-fated
MOO; and by Brian Murfin, a.k.a. Captain Bran Muffin, who has fearlessly
and tenaciously administered the actlab's many Internet nodes through rain,

sleet, dark of night, and the dreadful legion of patches necessitated by the introduction of new operating systems in the midst of ongoing projects— surely a task far beyond the call of duty.

2. Multiple-user social environments are described at length in Chapter 5.

3. There are plenty of predecessors to *Mines of Moria,* but they did not incorporate the elements of medieval role playing that were ubiquitous in all of the RPG games that followed. At MIT, by the 1960s the hackers of Project MAC had already written *Wumpus,* and when some of them moved on to Commodore and to Apple Computer in the mid-1970s, they immediately produced a version ported to the 6502 environment called *Hunt the Wumpus.* These could quite correctly be seen as earlier games of adventure, since they also incorporated the trademark Twisty Mazes, Dark Passages, Treasure, and of course the highly unpleasant Wumpus. What they lacked was the element of role playing, of engaging an *alter* persona, that characterized all the later games.

4. The term *handle* comes from amateur radio, where it means "nickname." On the Internet chat system *IRC,* the term is *nick.* In programming, a handle is a means (in practice, usually an address) by which a particular procedure or subroutine is reserved for use by a specific program.

5. In Van Gelder's account the psychiatrist used the name Joan Sue Greene.

6. Even in retrospect I find it astonishing that as late as 1983 significant numbers of people engaged in dialogue in virtual communities failed to grasp the problems raised by the existence of artificial personae. For many it was a nonissue. The level of concern was heavily gendered; when imposture became an issue, it was women who were most often hurt. This seems to be true because many women carried their social expectations regarding conversational style and confidentiality across the machinic boundary and into the virtual communities. To this extent they exemplified the conversational style that Lewin found so attractive.

7. At the time Stephen Hawking could still talk, after a fashion, and the keyboard-and-Votrax system that he would subsequently use had not yet been developed. Votraxes can speak in feminine intonation too, and such a system would have been perfect for Joan, had she existed.

8. A large amount of the distrust that began to surround Julie originated in the uncanny perfection of her relationship with John. Lewin had not taken into consideration the possibility of encountering a population of disabled persons on-line other than Julie, and has subsequently indicated that he might have modulated the Joan identity to allow for it. The "real" disabled women on-line were more conscious of the incongruity than was the chat system's general population; under the circumstances, it is not strange that

they viewed Julie's life first with joy and perhaps hope, then envy, and finally with deep suspicion.

9. And here, of course, the multiple meanings and uses of the term *apprehensible* become clear.

Chapter 4. *Reinvention and Encounter:* Pause for Theory

1. There is an implied intertextuality here with Glória Anzaldùa's project in the anthology *Making Face, Making Soul* (1990) that remains to be explored.

2. E.g., Strauss 1986; Sahlins 1976; Goffman 1963; Weber 1947; Lacan 1977; Booth 1983; Derrida 1978; Heidegger 1976; G. Stone 1962; Scheff and Shibutani 1986; A. Norman and Wiley 1986; Katovich 1986; Maines 1977.

3. Strauss alludes to Takashi Shibutani's work on reference group theory, which he quotes in his introduction to Strauss (1986, xxi).

4. Ibid.

5. In films made in the field, Strum demonstrated that when certain baboons felt threatened by a baboon higher in the hierarchy they would position themselves relative to a third baboon in such a way that the third baboon was between them and the more dominant baboon. This action defuses possible hostility from the dominant animal. Since the threatened baboon uses another member of the troop as an instrumentality such a strategy may be correctly called toolmaking.

6. I make no claims to understand their work better!

7. Ferguson (1990) dates the production of pleasure as a category of meaning from the transition from feudalism to capitalism, but, he notes, "It was only much later that pleasure became somewhat detached from reason and it was possible to imagine the latter as a process dependent upon the repression of the former. In fact it depended upon the repression of fun (as a separate category from pleasure) and through this the establishment of pleasure as a legitimate value for, and organizing principle of, personal and social life" (Ferguson 1990, 138).

8. Occasionally I am asked—quite reasonably, I think—how I happen to have data about such diverse areas as bandwidth and distortion with which to inform my fieldwork. The answer is that I happen to have done a lot of different things and was an observer at every stage. I tend to gloss over some of my research in the interest of getting on with the argument in which I happen to be interested, but because the discussion of distortion assumes a lot, I'm going to pause for a moment to fill in some background. I had begun

this work, quite unwittingly, much earlier while doing research for the American Foundation for the Blind. One of the main functions of the AFB is to record, manufacture, and distribute recorded books. For reasons of economy (records are heavy, shipping is expensive) the AFB was intensely interested in issues of bandwidth and data compression. I was specifically hired to research extremely slow disk recording techniques (turntable rotation speeds of 4 rpm and perhaps lower, compared to 33⅓ rpm) and high packing density (groove pitches of 600/in. and higher, compared to 200–400/in. for the average phonograph record). This work involves a large amount of experimentation with psychoacoustics, because at extremely low recording speeds distortion rises sharply, in the form of waveform degradation. (Finer pitch and slower speeds require smaller burnishing facets on the recording stylus, causing the contact area between groove and pickup stylus to diminish, plastic deformation of the vinyl to increase, and vertical excursions of the playback stylus at high frequencies to increase during playback. Low speed also reduces the polish on the groove surface, which lowers the high-frequency signal-to-noise ratio and increases the amount of heat generated by tracking, which in turn increases the rate of spalling. Spalling depends upon flow rates of the molten vinyl during the molding process; longer molding cycles at lower temperature reduce spalling, so there is a trade-off between economies of packing density and economies of manufacture.) Frequency variation characterized as wow and flutter is another form of distortion. (The stability of a rotating turntable expressed as the invariance of its angular velocity depends upon its mass times its angular velocity; at low speeds sufficient mass to stabilize rotation is impractical, so how much frequency variation can be tolerated by a listener under actual listening conditions becomes the issue of moment.) Obviously this is all history at this time, and nobody cares anymore because the CD instantly made it all irrelevant, and the people who did that work are no different from those wonderful folks who painstakingly figured out how to chip flint exquisitely well only to be deskilled by the unaesthetic fact of bronze, but that's not the point. In the course of the work I spent a lot of time in the archives, because the U.S. Navy had already done a great deal of research on how much and what kinds of distortion the human hearing mechanism can tolerate and what kinds of distortion are undetectable. Notice immediately the tie to military research even here, even here, in the gentle heart of the American Foundation for the Blind, right next door to the Margaret Sanger Institute in downtown Manhattan. The navy wanted to know these things in connection with speech intelligibility in air-to-ground and ground-to-ground battle intercommunication, and they had commissioned various studies (beginning in the 1940s: their own; Bolt, Beranek, and Newman; Bell Telephone Labs; Battelle Memorial Labs) to find out everything there was to know. By the time I finished with the navy's archives, with talking with everybody I could find who had done research on the subject, and with our own well-financed research, I had intimate knowledge of just about everything that had ever been done, said, whispered, thought, or imagined about issues of bandwidth and distortion. Consequently, when I walked into that collective of phone sex workers in 1985, it could be said that I was theoretically informed.

9. We might juxtapose Morningstar and Farmer's sanguine observation and its liberatory implications, made to an audience of programmers, with the problems of control experienced by the early designers of computer conferences, to foreground the particularity of institutional control and the locality of moral judgments in cyberspace—as well as in the communities that construct them.

10. Kenneth Haltmann (1990) points out that, in contrast to common belief, the earliest users of the telephone were uncomfortable with the idea of a voice coming out of a handset that one held to one's ear. In an interesting semiotic analysis of the physical structure of the telephone, Haltmann suggests that the original designers of the home phone constructed it with a deliberately anthropomorphic appearance. The quasi-human look of the instrument was meant to help ease the transition to electronically prostheticized speech by giving early users the sensation that they were speaking *to* the telephone instead of *through* it.

11. Note in passing the significant use of the word *on* to describe the relationship between agency and communication technology—on the air, on the phone—with which users of the technology seem far more comfortable than with the equally descriptive *in*. The use of *on* shows the same order of aversion to directly acknowledging the absence of proximate agency that may have underlain making early phones in quasi-human shape.

Chapter 5. *Agency and Proximity:* Communities/CommuniTrees

1. There is quite a bit of disagreement within the programming community about this statement. Many programmers feel that a page of uncommented C is about as opaque as a page of uncommented Forth. Occasionally the discussions become heated. So far I have not been swayed. I still observe that after considerable time programmers develop a kind of pattern recognition that enables the good ones to pick up a page of uncommented code in a structured language and get a fair idea of what is going on, and this ability is less common with Forth. Their interpretation may not tell them precisely what the code does, but it may be sufficient for some immediate purpose.

2. For reasons of simplicity in parsing, most programming languages re-

quire procedure names to consist of a single, unbroken string of characters. Programmers frequently use procedure names that are made up of several words, but they connect the words with the underbar character (_). This practice keeps the parser happy because it sees the underbar as just another character.

3. The opinion that "higher" languages such as C are generally more intelligible than Forth is not universally shared, and I have had some lively debates with fellow programmers about this premise. Perhaps it would be more useful to state that in my sample population the Forth programmers tended to be more radically eclectic in their approach to documentation and intelligibility than the programmers in languages such as C, Pascal, or Assembly. Of these, certainly assembly language lends itself most readily to crimes of unintelligibility, and perhaps for this very reason, the assembly language programmers in my sample population were the most conscientious documenters. This finding in turn suggests that there is some particular intentional quality shared by the Forth programmers in the sample that tends to produce more obscure documentation, and further suggests that the sample population should be enlarged; however, this possibility raises other issues which overcomplexify the study. To answer a possible unspoken question, by preference the author herself is an assembly language wonk who has also written successful commercial code in Pascal and C. For now, however, the study continues. . . . Stay tuned for a fascinating paper at its conclusion.

4. The spelling of *hir* was part of the Tree philosophy, which included ungendered language. Many utopian groups mounted attempts to create artificial ungendered pronouns (e.g., June Arnold's novel *The Cook and the Carpenter,* 1973), but none made it to mainstream use.

5. A significant footnote to this story is George Lucas's later recantation of the rebel mythos as it seemed to be described in *Star Wars.* Lucas stated that in *Return of the Jedi* the rebel forces ultimately won not because of their better maneuverability and individual initiative, but because they possessed technically superior weapons. Lucas seems to have wanted to send a message to potential rebels of any stripe that skill and pluck alone do not win battles in the late twentieth century—a lesson that inner-city gangs, who have rapidly appropriated high-technology weaponry to kill themselves, each other, and anyone who happens to be nearby, have taken to heart.

6. It is not clear whether the tree gods got this phrase from Stewart Brand, or vice versa. Its articulation was a natural part of the prevailing techno-epistemology in northern California during this period.

7. A tremendous amount of otherwise useful time is still spent in simply convincing the majority of faculty in traditional communications studies

programs that this statement is true. To take an example from close to home, as of this writing (February 1993) at least one graduate student of my acquaintance is still attempting to convince his dissertation advisers not that virtual communities are worthy subjects for extensive research, but simply that they exist.

8. The trivial cases to which I refer are occasional attempts by businesses to limit prosthetic communication in the workplace to that which is necessary to carry out corporate agendas.

9. In my lab at the University of Texas a group of researchers has built a MOO that is a model of Austin and that possesses a kind of gritty reality reminiscent of something that might have been dreamed up by Bruce Sterling on cheap bourbon. Like many MOOs, including MediaMOO, PointMOOt runs on top of Curtis's LambdaCore code.

10. I don't want to belabor points about Japanese culture, nor particularly to unpack them, as this essay has other purposes. Of course the situation in Japan is more complex than the limited exposition I provide here would make it seem, and far more goes on beneath the smooth social surface of Japanese culture, but these activities do not yet take the form of social formations visible to this gaijin.

Chapter 6. *The End of Innocence, Part I:* Cyberdämmerung at the Atari Lab

1. Myron Krueger, whose 1977 dissertation "Artificial Reality" was a foundational text for the field, is less frequently mentioned in later accounts, although he is still an active researcher. By choosing to pursue a research style which is frequently identified as art rather than technobusiness, Krueger's seminal work frequently falls outside the hot scramble for control and the concomitant high-stakes profits in the emerging cyberspace industries—or so the conglomerates now battling for a piece of the interactive pie seem to believe.

This chapter incorporates material from a larger study, still under way, of the rise and fall of the first generation of Silicon Valley laboratories conducting research into interaction and presence. Data collection is still in progress, but so far the chapter as presented here includes material from conversations with Brenda Laurel, Scott Fisher, Michael Naimark, Steve Gano, Alan Kay, Susan Brennan, Douglas Crockford, Eric Hulteen, and Eric Gullichsen. In experimenting with various ways of presenting the material, I have chosen to combine the styles of several researchers whose work, I felt, conveyed the sense of events I wanted for the Atari piece. These include

Frank Rose, from his early study of the Silicon Valley technospiritual movement *Wired to God* and his later study of "the end of innocence at Apple Computer," *West of Eden* (1989). Gary Taubes' *Nobel Dreams* (1986), a study of the discovery of the W and Z particles by a segment of the high-energy physics community, was also useful, as was the work of Leo Tolstoy (because, after all, I had to).

2. The history of the development of computational devices is littered with Xerox's missed opportunities, as the scientists and engineers at PARC came up with one brilliant, marketable product after another . . . all of which Xerox ignored. When Xerox's seemingly endless profitability began to fade in the late 1970s, it was too late. For an excellent study of this rolling disaster, see *Fumbling the Future at Xerox* (Smith 1988).

3. Laurel was also ABD in theater criticism. Her work at the lab on "interactive fantasy systems," together with her association with Alan Kay, led to her dissertation, which she completed in 1986.

4. During my sojourn in San Diego I mentioned to Bruno Latour that any consideration of how a commercially produced object came to possess agency would inevitably require some theorizing about the Mafia. "Ridiculous," Latour said.

5. Kay now feels that he was misquoted or misunderstood in the meeting. "What I said," he maintains, "was that they were going to commit a *seemingly* infinite amount."

6. Chip manufacturers only provide technical support for characteristics of their chips that appear in the published specifications. If a coder were to find an unpublished instruction built into a chip that made it run ten times faster and whistle "Dixie" at the same time, the manufacturer would still not support it.

7. Space does not allow a good explanation of the intricacies of self-modifying code, which, in brief, rewrites itself as it runs. Under certain circumstances this hack can produce extremely compact code that serves several different purposes with the same routines. Respectable programmers hate it, because it is almost impossible to debug. Obviously it is extremely popular among machine language wonks.

8. Susan Leigh Star and Donna Haraway have both written about the idea of boundary objects. In her Paper Tiger video *Donna Haraway Reads National Geographic* (1986), Haraway describes the jungle family of Tarzan, Jane, and their chimp "child" as boundary objects who inhabit the intersections of multiple social categories, and by this means complexly blur or "queer" them. Star has written more extensively on boundary objects as discursive constructs that look different to different observers and thus can

be used to translate knowledge across incommensurable domains (Star 1989; Star and Griesemer 1989).

9. These are laid out in more detail in Stuart Brand's *The Media Lab: Inventing the Future at MIT* (1987), which is an excellent look at the early interactivists.

10. Although Stein made no comment at the time, Laurel was subsequently bounced from the project. It is worth noting that after several more incarnations, Laurel and Stein have become friends. Stein has gone on to do groundbreaking work on interactivity at Voyager, one of the first publishers of interactive software.

11. If it needs belaboring, the joke is "O.fischell." Arthur and Olivia also had two kids, Super and Benny.

12. The term "Jabba the Hutt" was first used, appropriately enough, by a group from LucasFilm that was visiting Atari on an exploratory mission to see what the two companies might have in common in regard to interactivity research.

Bibliography

Alexander, V. K. 1956. A case study of multiple personality. *Journal of Abnormal and Social Psychology* 52:272–276.

Allan, Francis. 1984. The end of intimacy. *Human Rights,* Winter 1984, p. 55.

Allison, R. B. 1984. The possession syndrome on trial. *American Journal of Forensic Psychiatry* 6:46–56.

Anzaldùa, Glória. 1987. *Borderlands/La Frontera: The New Mestiza.* San Francisco: Spinsters/Aunt Lute.

———. (ed.). 1990. *Making Face, Making Soul Haciendo Caras: Creative and Critical Perspectives by Feminists of Color.* San Francisco: Aunt Lute.

Arnold, June. 1973. *The Cook and the Carpenter: A Novel by the Carpenter.* Plainfield, VT: Daughters.

Ashmore, Malcolm. 1989. *The Reflexive Thesis: Wrighting Sociology of Scientific Knowledge.* Foreword by Steve Woolgar. Chicago: University of Chicago Press.

Atwood, G. E. 1978. The impact of Sybil on a person with multiple personality. *American Journal of Psychoanalysis* 38:277–279.

Barker, Francis. 1984. *The Tremulous Private Body: Essays in Subjection.* London: Methuen.

Baudrillard, Jean. 1987. *The Ecstasy of Communication,* trans. Bernard and Caroline Schutze, ed. Sylvere Lotringer. New York: Semiotext(e).

Binet, A. 1977. *On Double Consciousness.* Washington, DC: University Publications of America.

Brand, Stewart. 1987. *The Media Lab: Inventing the Future at MIT.* New York: Viking.

Breuer, J., and Freud, S. 1986 (1895). *Studies in Hysteria.* New York: Pelican Books.

Bush, Vannevar. 1945. Bush report on scientific research in the United States. Washington, DC: Public Affairs Press.

————. 1946. *Endless Horizons.* Introduction by Dr. Frank B. Jewett. Washington, DC: Public Affairs Press.

Butler, Judith. 1990. *Gender Trouble: Feminism and the Subversion of Identity.* New York: Routledge.

Campbell, Joseph. 1959. *The Masks of God: Primitive Mythology.* New York: Viking.

Certeau, Michel de. 1985. The arts of dying: Celibatory machines. In *Heterologies,* trans. Brian Massumi. Minneapolis: University of Minnesota Press.

Clark, E. E. 1960. *Indian Legends of the Pacific Northwest.* Toronto: McClelland and Stewart.

Clifford, James. 1986. *Writing Culture: The Poetics and Politics of Ethnography: A School of American Research Advanced Seminar,* ed. James Clifford and George E. Marcus. Berkeley: University of California Press.

————. 1988. *The Predicament of Culture: Twentieth-Century Ethnography, Literature, and Art.* Cambridge, MA: Harvard University Press.

Cohn, Carol. 1987. Sex and death in the rational world of defense intellectuals. *Signs: Journal of Woman in Culture and Society* 12:4.

Collins, Harry. 1985. *Changing Order: Replication and Induction in Scientific Practice.* London: Sage.

De Landa, Manuel. 1991. *War in the Age of Intelligent Machines.* Swerve eds. New York: Zone Books.

Delany, Samuel R. 1979. *Tales of Neveryon.* New York: Bantam.

Deleuze, Gilles, and Felix Guattari. 1983. *Anti-Oedipus: Capitalism and Schizophrenia.* Translated from the French by Robert Hurley, Mark Seem, and Helen R. Lane. Preface by Michel Foucuault. Minneapolis: University of Minnesota Press.

————. 1987. *A Thousand Plateaus: Capitalism and Schizophrenia.* Translation and foreword by Brian Massumi. Minneapolis: University of Minnesota Press.

Dewey, John. 1981 (1896). The reflex arc concept in psychology. In J. J. McDermott (ed.), *The Philosophy of John Dewey,* pp. 136–148. Chicago: University of Chicago Press.

Drexler, K. Eric. 1986. *Engines of Creation.* Foreword by Marvin Minsky. Garden City, NY: Anchor Press/Doubleday.

Dunlop, Charles, and Robert Kling (eds.). *Computerization and Controversy: Value Conflicts and Social Choices.* Boston: Academic Press.

Edwards, Paul N. 1986. Artificial intelligence and high-technology war: The perspective of the formal machine. *Silicon Valley Research Group Working Paper No. 6* (unpub.).

Eliade, M. 1964. *Shamanism*. Princeton, NJ: Princeton University Press.

Epstein, Julie, and Kristina Straub (eds.). 1991. *Body Guards: The Cultural Politics of Gender Ambiguity*. New York: Routledge.

Ferguson, Harvie. 1990. *The Science of Pleasure*. London: Routledge.

Foucault, Michel. 1965. *Madness and Civilization: A History of Insanity in the Age of Reason*, trans. Richard Howard. New York: Pantheon.

————. 1971. *The Order of Things*. New York: Pantheon.

————. 1977. *Discipline and Punish: The Birth of the Prison*, trans. Alan Sheridan. New York: Pantheon.

Geertz, Clifford. 1973. *The Interpretation of Cultures* (collection). New York: Basic Books.

Gibson, William. 1984. *Neuromancer*. New York: Ace.

Goodeve, Thyrza Nichols. 1989. The horror of no longer remembering the reason for forgetting, or "When the time comes for our battle, the memories'll be the armor." *Art Forum*, special issue, "Wonder," Summer 1989.

Habermas, J. 1979. *Communication and the Evolution of Society*. Boston: Beacon Press.

Haltmann, Kenneth. 1990. Reaching out to touch someone? Reflections on the semiotics of a 1923 candlestick telephone. *Technology and Society* 12:333–354.

Haraway, Donna. 1985. A manifesto for cyborgs: Science, technology and socialist feminism in the 1980s. *Socialist Review* 80:65–107.

————. 1989. The biopolitics of postmodern bodies: Determinations of self and other in immune system discourse. *Differences* 1:1.

————. 1990. *Private Visions: Gender, Race and Nature in the World of Modern Science*. New York: Routledge.

————. 1991a. Cyborgs at large: An interview with Donna Haraway. In Constance Penley and Andrew Ross (eds.), *Technoculture*. Minneapolis: University of Minnesota Press.

————. 1991b. The promises of monsters: A regenerative politics for inappropriate/d others. In Paula Treichler and Gary Nelson (eds.), *Cultural Studies*. New York: Routledge.

————. 1991c. *Simians, Cyborgs, and Women: The Reinvention of Nature* (collected essays). New York: Routledge.

————. 1991d. The subjects are cyborg, nature is Coyote, and the geography is elsewhere: Postscript to "Cyborgs at Large." In Constance Penley and Andrew Ross (eds.), *Technoculture*. Minneapolis: University of Minnesota Press.

Harner, M. J. (ed.). 1973. *Hallucinogens and Shamanism*. New York: Oxford University Press.

Hayles, N. Katherine. 1987a. Text out of context: Situating postmodernism within an information society. *Discourse* 9:24–36.

————. 1987b. Denaturalizing experience: Postmodern literature and science. Abstract from the conference Literature and Science as Modes of Expression, sponsored by the Society for Literature and Science, October 8–11, Worcester Polytechnic Institute.

Head, Henry. 1920. *Studies in Neurology*. Oxford: The University Press.

————. 1926. *Aphasia and Kindred Disorders of Speech*. Cambridge: The University Press; New York: Macmillan.

Heim, Michael. 1991. The erotic ontology of cyperspace. In Michael Benedikt (ed.), *Cyberspace: First Steps*. Cambridge, MA: MIT Press.

Hewitt, Carl. 1977a. Viewing control structures as patterns of passing messages. *Artificial Intelligence* 8:323–364.

————. 1977b. The challenge of open systems. *Byte* 10 (April).

Huyssen, Andreas. 1986. *After the Great Divide: Modernism, Mass Culture, Postmodernism*. Bloomington: Indiana University Press.

Jakobson, Roman. 1971. *Selected Writings 2*. The Hague: Mouton.

James, William. 1904. *The Principles of Psychology*, 2 vols. New York: Henry Holt.

Jameson, Fredric. 1981. On interpretation: Literature as a socially symbolic act. In *The Political Unconscious*. Ithaca, NY: Cornell University Press.

————. 1991. *Postmodernism: The Cultural Logic of Late Capitalism* (collected essays). Durham, NC: Duke University Press.

Jones, Ernest. 1953. *The Life and Work of Sigmund Freud*. New York: Basic Books.

Katovich, Michael, 1986. Temporal stages of situated activity and identity activation. In Carl J. Couch, Stanley L. Saxton, and Michael A. Katovich (eds.), *Studies in Symbolic Interaction: The Iowa School*. Greenwich, CT: JAI Press.

Kellogg, Wendy, John M. Carroll, and John T. Richards. 1991. Making reality a cyberspace. In Michael Benedikt (ed.), *Cyberspace: First Steps.* Cambridge, MA: MIT Press.

Kristeva, Julia. 1973. The system and the speaking subject. *Times Literary Supplement,* October 12.

Kristeva, Julia, J. Rey-Dubove, and D. J. Umiker. 1971. *Essays in Semiotics.* The Hague: Mouton.

Kroeber, A. L. 1952. *The Nature of Culture.* Chicago: University of Chicago Press.

Krueger, Myron W. 1983. *Artificial Reality.* Reading, MA: Addison-Wesley.

————. 1983. *Artificial Reality II.* Reading, MA: Addison-Wesley.

Lacan, Jacques. 1968. *The Language of the Self: The Function of Language in Psychoanalysis,* trans. Anthony Wilden. New York: Dell.

————. 1977. *The Four Fundamental Concepts of Psychoanalysis,* trans. Alain Sheridan, ed. Jacques-Alain Miller. London: Hogarth.

LaPorte, T. R. (ed). 1975. *Organized Social Complexity: Challenge to Politics and Policy.* Princeton, NJ: Princeton University Press.

Latour, Bruno. 1988. *The Pasteurization of France.* Cambridge, MA: Harvard University Press.

————. 1990. On actor-network theory: A few clarifications plus more than a few complications.

Laurel, Brenda. 1982. The poetics of interactive form. *Atari Research Memo #17,* December 10, 1982.

————. 1984. First-personess in interface design (co-authored with Eric A. Hulteen). *Atari Research Memo #22,* January 23, 1984.

————. 1986a. Interface as mimesis. In D. A. Norman and S. Draper (eds.), *User Centered System Design: New Perspectives on Human-Computer Interaction.* Hillsdale, NJ: Lawrence Erlbaum Associates, 1986.

————. 1986b. Toward the design of a computer-based interactive fantasy system. Ph.D. Dissertation, The Ohio State University, 1986.

————. 1987. Reassessing interactivity. *The Journal of Computer Game Design* 1(3): 7–10.

————. 1988. Culture hacking. *The Journal of Computer Game Design* 1(8): 4–5.

————. 1989a. On dramatic interaction. *Verbum, Journal of Personal Computer Aesthetics* 3(3).

————. 1989b. Games women play: Some alternative approaches. *The Journal of Computer Game Design* 2(5).

————. 1989c. New interfaces for entertainment. *The Journal of Computer Game Design* 2(4).

————. 1989d. A taxonomy of interactive movies. *New Media News* 3(1): 5–8.

————. 1990a. *The Art of Human–Computer Interface Design.* Reading, MA: Addison-Wesley.

————. 1990b. Virtual reality design: A personal view. *Multimedia Review,* Summer 1990.

————. 1991a. Art and activism in VR. *Verbum, Journal of Personal Computer Aesthetics* 5(2).

————. 1991b. Global media and common ground. *Verbum Interactive 1.0,* May 1991.

————. 1991c. Strange new worlds of entertainment. *Compute,* November 1991.

————. 1992a. Artistic frontiers in virtual reality. *SIGGRAPH '92 Catalog,* July 1992.

————. 1992b. Global media and cultural diversity. *TISEA Catalog,* November 1992.

————. 1992c. Issues in multimedia interface design: Media integration and interface agents. Brenda Laurel, Tim Oren, and Abbe Don. *Proceedings of CHI '90* (ACM SIGCHI). April 1990. Reprinted in M. Blattner and R. Dannenerg (eds.), *Multimedia Interface Design.* ACM Press/Addison-Wesley.

————. 1993a. *Computers as Theatre.* Reading, MA: Addison-Wesley.

————. 1993b. Immersion technologies. *Wired,* December 1993.

————. 1993c. Kids online: Do something constructive! *Edutopia, Newsletter of the George Lucas Education Foundation,* Winter 1993.

————. 1994a. Placeholder: Landscape and narrative in virtual environments, with Rachel Strickland and Rob Tow. *Computer Graphics,* 28(2): 118–126.

————. 1994b. Placeholder: Real bodies in virtual worlds, with Rob Tow. *Proceedings of the Computer Game Developers' Conference,* April 1994, San Jose, CA.

Le Guin, Ursula K. 1985. *Always Coming Home,* composer, Todd Barton; artist, Margaret Chodos; geomancer, George Hersh; maps drawn by the author. New York: Harper & Row.

Lehman-Wilzig, Sam. 1981. Frankenstein unbound: Toward a legal definition of artificial intelligence. *Futures,* December 1981, p. 447.

Levine, Steven. 1988. *Who Dies? An Investigation of Conscious Living and Conscious Dying.* Bath: Gateway.

Lewis, I. M. 1971. *Ecstatic Religion: An Anthropological Study of Spirit Possession and Shamanism.* Baltimore: Penguin Books.

Ludolph, P. S. 1985. How prevalent is multiple personality? (And reply of E. L. Bliss.) Letters to the Editor, *American Journal of General Psychiatry* 26:298–310.

Luria, A. R. 1987 (1968). *The Mind of a Mnemonist.* Cambridge, MA: Harvard University Press.

Luria, A. R. 1987 (1972). *The Man with a Shattered World.* Cambridge, MA: Harvard University Press.

McFadden, Tim. 1991. The structure of cyberspace and the ballistic actors model. In Michael Benedikt (ed.), *Cyberspace: First Steps.* Cambridge, MA: MIT Press.

Mead, George Herbert. 1934. *Mind, Self and Society,* ed. C. W. Morris. Chicago: University of Chicago Press.

———. 1977 (1956 posth.). *On Social Psychology,* introduction by Anselm Strauss. Chicago: University of Chicago Press.

Mercer, Kobena, et al. 1988. *Black Film, British Cinema.* London: Institute of Contemporary Arts.

Merleau-Ponty, Maurice. 1962. *Phenomenology of Perception,* trans. Colin Smith. New York: Humanities Press.

———. 1964a. *Sense and Non-Sense,* trans. Hubert L. Dreyfus and Patricia Allen Dreyfus. Chicago: Northwestern University Press.

———. 1964b. *Signs,* trans. Richard McCleary. Chicago: Northwestern University Press.

Mitchell, Silas Weir, George Read Morehouse, and William Williams Keen. 1864 (1989). *Gunshot Wounds and Other Injuries of Nerves,* reprinted with biographical introductions by Ira M. Rutkow. American Civil War Surgery Series, vol. 3. San Francisco: Norman.

———. 1872 (1965). *Injuries of Nerves and Their Consequences,* with a new introduction by Lawrence C. McHenry, Jr. American Academy of Neurology Reprint Series, vol. 2. New York: Dover.

Morningstar, Chip, and F. Randall Farmer. 1991. The lessons of Lucasfilm's Habitat. In Michael Benedikt (ed.), *Cyberspace: First Steps.* Cambridge, MA: MIT Press.

Noddings, Nel. 1984. *Caring: A Feminine Approach to Ethics and Moral Education.* Berkeley: University of California Press.

Norman, Alexander C., and Mary Glenn Wiley. 1986. *Situated Activity and Identity Formation.*

Norman, Donald. 1990. *The Design of Everyday Things.* (Previous title: *The Psychopathology of Everyday Things.*) Reading, MA: Addison-Wesley.

Novak, Marcos. 1991. Liquid architectures in cyberspace. In Michael Benedikt (ed.), *Cyberspace: First Steps.* Cambridge, MA: MIT Press.

Peirce, Charles Sanders. 1931–58. *Collected Papers,* vols. 1–6, ed. C. Hartshorne and P. Weiss; vols. 7–8, ed. A. W. Burks. Cambridge, MA: Harvard University Press.

Putnam, F. W. 1985. Dissociation as a response to extreme trauma. In R. P. Kluft (ed.), *Childhood Antecedents of Multiple Personality Disorder.* Washington, DC: American Psychiatric Press.

———. 1988. The switch process in multiple personality disorder. *Dissociation* 1:24–32.

Quen, Jacques M. (ed). 1984. *Split Minds/Split Brains: Historical and Current Perspectives.* New York: New York University Press.

Rabinow, Paul. 1977. *Reflections on Fieldwork in Morocco.* Berkeley: University of California Press.

———. 1991. From sociobiology to biosociality: Artificiality and enlightenment. In *Zone 6: Fragments for a History of the Body,* vol. 4: *Incorporations.* New York: Urzone (MIT).

Reid, Roddey. 1993. *Families in Jeopardy: Regulating the Social Body in France, 1750–1910.* Stanford, CA: Stanford University Press.

Rentmeister, Cacilia. 1976. Beruftsverbot fur Musen. *Aesthetik und Kommunikation* 25 (September): 92–112.

Roberts, Mary Louise. 1994. *Civilization Without Sexes: Reconstructing Gender in Postwar France, 1917–1927.* Chicago: University of Chicago Press.

Roheim, Geza. 1928. Early stages of the Oedipus complex. *International Journal of Psycho-analysis* 9.

———. 1947. Dream analysis and field work in anthropology. *Psychoanalysis and the Social Sciences.* New York: International Universities Press.

Rose, Frank. 1984. Wired to God. *Vanity Fair,* May.

———. 1989. *West of Eden: The End of Innocence at Apple Computer.* New York: Viking.

Ross, Colin A. 1986. *Multiple Personality Disorder: Diagnosis, Clinical Features, and Treatment.* New York: John Wiley & Sons.

Sahlins, Marshall. 1976. *Culture and Practical Reason.* Chicago: University of Chicago Press.

Scarry, Elaine. 1985. *The Body in Pain: The Making and Unmaking of the World.* New York: Oxford University Press.

Scheff, Thomas J. 1990. *Microsociology: Discourse, Emotion, and Social Structure.* Chicago: University of Chicago Press.

———, and Shibutani (eds.). 1986. *Human Nature and Collective Behavior.*

Shapin, Steven, and Simon Schaffer. 1985. *Leviathan and the Air-Pump: Hobbes, Boyle, and the Experimental Life.* Princeton, NJ: Princeton University Press.

Shaviro, Steven. 1993. *The Cinematic Body.* Minneapolis: University of Minnesota Press.

Singer, Milton. 1984. *Man's Glassy Essence: Explorations in Semiotic Anthropology.* Bloomington: Indiana University Press.

Smith, Douglas K. 1988. *Fumbling the Future: How Xerox Invented, Then Ignored, the First Personal Computer.* New York: Morrow.

Sobchak, Vivian Carol. 1987. *Screening Space: The American Science Fiction Film,* 2nd, enl. ed. New York: Ungar.

———. 1988. The scene of the screen: Toward a phenomenology of cinematic and electronic "presence." In H. V. Gumbrecht and L. K. Pfeiffer (eds.), *Materialitat des Kommunikation.* GDR: Suhrkarp-Verlag.

———. 1991. *The Address of the Eye: A Semiotic Phenomenology of Cinematic Embodiment.* Princeton, NJ: Princeton University Press.

Sprengnether, Madelon. 1985. *The (M)other Tongue: Essays in Feminist Psychoanalytic Interpretation,* ed. Shirley Nelson Garner, Claire Kahane, and Madelon Sprengnether. Ithaca, NY: Cornell University Press.

———. 1990. *The Spectral Mother: Freud, Feminism, and Psychoanalysis.* Ithaca, NY: Cornell University Press.

Star, Susan Leigh. 1989. The structure of ill-structured solutions: Heterogeneous problem-solving, boundary objects and distributed artificial intelligence. In M. Huhns and L. Gasser (eds.), *Distributed Artificial Intelligence 2,* pp. 37–54. Menlo Park: Morgan Kauffmann.

———, and James Griesemer. 1989. Institutional ecology, "translations," and coherence: Amateurs and professionals in Berkeley's Museum of Vertebrate Zoology, 1907–1939. *Social Studies of Science,* 19:387–420.

Starhawk. 1989. *The Spiral Dance: A Rebirth of the Ancient Religion of the*

Great Goddess, 10th anniv. ed., with new introduction and commentary. San Francisco: Harper & Row.

Stephenson, Neal. 1992. *Snow Crash.* New York: Bantam Spectra.

Stewart, W. A. 1984. Analytic biography of Anna O. In M. Rosenbaum and M. Muroff (eds.), *Anna O.: Fourteen Contemporary Reinterpretations.* New York: Free Press.

Stoller, R. J. 1973. *Splitting: A Case of Female Masculinity.* New York: Dell.

Stone, Allucquère Rosanne (as Sandy Stone). 1991a. The empire strikes back: A posttranssexual manifesto. In Kristina Straub and Julia Epstein (eds.), *Body Guards: The Cultural Politics of Gender Ambiguity.* New York: Routledge.

————. 1991b. Will the real body please stand up?: Boundary stories about virtual cultures. In Michael Benedikt (ed.), *Cyberspace: First Steps.* Cambridge, MA: MIT Press.

————. 1992a. The architecture of elsewhere. In Hrazstan Zeitlian (ed.), *Semiotext(e) Architecture.* New York: Semiotext(e).

————. 1992b. Virtual systems. In Jonathan Crary and Stanford Kwinter (eds.), *Zone 6: Incorporations,* Vol. 6 of *Fragments for a History of the Human Body.* New York: Urzone (MIT).

———— (as Sandy Stone). 1993a. The *empire* strikes back: A posttranssexual manifesto. Revised and updated from the original 1991 version. *Camera Obscura 26.*

————. 1993b. Virtualitet og Krenkelser. Norwegian translation of "Violation and virtuality: Two cases of physical and psychological boundary transgression and their implications." In Terje Rasmussen (ed.), *Kulturens Digitale.* Oslo: Aventura Forlag A/S.

————. 1994a. Invaginal imaginal: How to fill (or surround) virtual space. Facing-page French translation as "Imaginaire Invaginal." In Lillian Lenox (ed.), *Lusitania: Special Issue: Vulvamorphia.* New York: Autonomedia.

————. 1994b. Sex, death, and architecture. *Architecture New York (ANY).* Special issue for the Guggenheim/ANY colloquium *Electrotecture.* New York: Anyone Press.

————. 1994c. Split subjects, not atoms; or how I fell in love with my prosthesis. In Mario Biagioli, Roddey Reid, and Sharon Traweek (eds.), *Configurations,* Special Issue on "Located Knowledges: Intersections between Cultural, Gender, and Science Studies." Baltimore: Johns Hopkins University Press.

————. 1994d. What vampires know: Transsubjection and transgender in cyberspace. Facing-page German translation as "Was Vampire wissen: Von transitiven Subjekten und Geschlectem in virtuellen Welten," illustrated. In Eva Ursprung (ed.), *In Control: Mensch-Interface-Maschine.* Graz: Kunstverein W.A.S.

———. 1995a. Computers and communication (with Nikhil Sinha). In John Downing (ed.), *Communication and Culture.* London: Sage.

———. 1995b. Innocence and awakening: Cyberdämmerung at the Ashibe Research Lab. In George Marcus (ed.), *Conversations, Profits and Memoirs,* Vol. II of *Late Editions: Cultural Studies for the End of the Century.* Chicago: University of Chicago Press.

———. 1995c. Sex and death among the disembodied: VR, cyberspace, and the nature of academic discourse. In S. L. Star (ed.), *The Culture of Computing.* London: Verso.

———. 1995d. Transsexual lesbian bikers abducted by space aliens and forced to watch Tab Hunter reruns—Film at eleven! In Crystal Gray (ed.), *The Cyborg Handbook.* New York: Routledge.

Stone, Christopher D. 1974. *Should Trees Have Standing?—Toward Legal Rights for Natural Objects.* New York: William A. Kaufman.

Stone, Gregory P. 1962. Appearances of the self. In Arnold M. Rose (ed.), *Human Behavior and Social Processes.* Boston: Houghton Mifflin.

Strauss, Anselm, ed. 1986. *G. H. Mead on Social Psychology.* Chicago: University of Chicago Press.

Strum, Shirley C. 1987. *Almost Human: A Journey into the World of Baboons.* Drawings by Deborah Ross. New York: Random House.

Taubes, Gary. 1986. *Nobel Dreams: Power, Deceit, and the Ultimate Experiment.* New York: Random House.

Theweleit, Klaus. 1977. *Male Fantasies,* vol. 1. Frankfurt am Main: Verlag Roter Stern.

Tomas, David. 1989. The technophilic body: On technicity in William Gibson's cyborg culture. *New Formations* 8 (Spring).

Traweek, Sharon. 1988. *Beamtimes and Lifetimes: The World of High-Energy Physicists.* Cambridge, MA: Harvard University Press.

Tuan, Yi-fu. 1982. *Segmented Worlds and Self: Group Life and Individual Consciousness.* Minneapolis: University of Minnesota Press.

Turkle, Sherry. 1984. *The Second Self: Computers and the Human Spirit.* New York: Simon and Schuster.

———. 1993. Constructions and reconstructions of the self in virtual reality.

Paper presented at 3Cyberconf: The Third International Conference on Cyberspace, Austin, Texas.

Van Gelder, Lindsy. 1985. The strange case of the electronic lover. *Ms.,* October, pp. 94–95.

Varley, John. 1986. *Blue Champagne.* New York: Berkley.

Virilio, Paul. 1991a. *The Aesthetics of Disappearance,* trans. Philip Beitchman. New York: Semiotext(e).

Virilio, Paul. 1991b. *Lumière de la vitesse.*

Von Foerster, Heinz (ed.). 1951. *Transactions of the Conference on Cybernetics.* New York: Josiah Macy, Jr., Foundation.

Weiner, Norbert. 1950. *The Human Use of Human Beings.* New York: Avon.

Wexelblat, Alan. 1991. Up two and over one: The semantic of dimension. In Michael Benedikt (ed.), *Cyberspace: First Steps.* Cambridge, MA: MIT Press.

Wilbur, C. B. 1984. Multiple personality and child abuse. *Psychiatric Clinics of North America* 7:3–7.

Wilden, Anthony. 1980. *System and Structure: Essays in Communication and Exchange,* 2nd ed. New York: Routledge Chapman & Hall (Tavistock).

Wilson, Kevin G. 1988. *Technologies of Control: The New Interactive Media for the Home.* Madison: University of Wisconsin Press.

Winograd, T., and F. Flores. 1986. *Understanding Computers and Cognition: A New Foundation for Design.* Norwood, NJ: Ablex.

Young, W. C. 1987. Emergence of a multiple personality disorder in post-traumatic stress disorder of adulthood. *American Journal of Clinical Hypnosis* 26:249–254.